# TACHS Skill Practice!

Test for Admission into
Catholic High Schools
Practice Test Questions

Copyright © 2013 by Complete Test Preparation Inc.
ALL RIGHTS RESERVED. No part of this book may be reproduced or transferred in any form or by any means, graphic, electronic, or mechanical, including photocopying, recording, web distribution, taping, or by any information storage retrieval system, without the written permission of the author.

Notice: Complete Test Preparation Inc. makes every reasonable effort to obtain from reliable sources accurate, complete, and timely information about the tests covered in this book. Nevertheless, changes can be made in the tests or the administration of the tests at any time and Complete Test Preparation Inc. makes no representation or warranty, either expressed or implied as to the accuracy, timeliness, or completeness of the information contained in this book. Complete Test Preparation Inc. makes no representations or warranties of any kind, express or implied, about the completeness, accuracy, reliability, suitability or availability with respect to the information contained in this document for any purpose. Any reliance you place on such information is therefore strictly at your own risk.

The author(s) shall not be liable for any loss incurred as a consequence of the use and application, directly or indirectly, of any information presented in this work. Sold with the understanding, the author(s) is not engaged in rendering professional services or advice. If advice or expert assistance is required, the services of a competent professional should be sought.

The company, product and service names used in this publication are for identification purposes only. All trademarks and registered trademarks are the property of their respective owners. Complete Test Preparation Inc. is not affiliated with any educational institution.

**We strongly recommend that students check with exam providers for up-to-date information regarding test content.**

Published by
Complete Test Preparation Inc.
Victoria BC Canada
Visit us on the web at https://www.test-preparation.ca
Printed in the USA

Version 7.5 - January 2018

## About Complete Test Preparation Inc.

The Complete Test Preparation Team has been publishing high quality study materials since 2005. Over one million students visit our websites every year, and thousands of students, teachers and parents all over the world (over 100 countries) have purchased our teaching materials, curriculum, study guides and practice tests.

Complete Test Preparation is committed to providing students with the best study materials and practice tests available on the market. Members of our team combine years of teaching experience, with experienced writers and editors, all with advanced degrees.

**ISBN-13: 9781772450941**

Complete Test Preparation is not affiliated with the makers of the TACHS, who do not endorse this product.

# Feedback

We welcome your feedback. Email us at feedback@test-preparation.ca with your comments and suggestions. We carefully review all suggestions and often incorporate reader suggestions into upcoming versions. As a Print on Demand Publisher, we update our products frequently.

 **Find us on Facebook**

WWW.FACEBOOK.COM / COMPLETETESTPREPARATION

# Contents

**6** **Getting Started**
   The TACHS® Study Plan          7
   Making a Study Schedule        7

**13** **Practice Test Questions Set 1**
   Answer Key                     81

**106** **Practice Test Questions Set 2**
   Answer Key                     170

**194** **Conclusion**

**195** **Multiple Choice Secrets Special Offer**

# Getting Started

CONGRATULATIONS! By deciding to take the Test for Admission into Catholic High Schools (TACHS®), you have taken the first step toward a great future! Of course, there is no point in taking this important examination unless you intend to do your best to earn the highest grade you possibly can. That means getting yourself organized and discovering the best approaches, methods and strategies to master the material. Yes, that will require real effort and dedication on your part, but if you are willing to focus your energy and devote the study time necessary, before you know it you will be opening a letter of acceptance to the school of your choice!

We know that taking on a new endeavour can be a little scary, and it is easy to feel unsure of where to begin. That's where we come in. This study guide is designed to help you improve your test-taking skills, show you a few tricks of the trade and increase both your competency and confidence.

## The Test for Admission into Catholic High School TACHS

The TACHS exam is composed of four sections, section one, Reading, comprises vocabulary, and reading comprehension, section two is English language. Section three is mathematics and section four is Ability, or IQ.

While we seek to make our guide as comprehensive as possible, note that like all exams, the TACHS Exam might be adjusted at some future point. New material might be added, or content that is no longer relevant or applicable might be removed. It is always a good idea to give the materials you receive when you register to take the TACHS® a careful review.

# The TACHS® Study Plan

Now that you have made the decision to take the TACHS®, it is time to get started. Before you do another thing, you will need to figure out a plan of attack. The very best study tip is to start early! The longer the time period you devote to regular study practice, the more likely you will be to retain the material and be able to access it quickly. If you thought that 1x20 is the same as 2x10, guess what? It really is not, when it comes to study time. Reviewing material for just an hour per day over the course of 20 days is far better than studying for two hours a day for only 10 days. The more often you revisit a particular piece of information, the better you will know it. Not only will your grasp and understanding be better, but your ability to reach into your brain and quickly and efficiently pull out the tidbit you need, will be greatly enhanced as well.

The great Chinese scholar and philosopher Confucius believed that true knowledge could be defined as knowing both what you know and what you do not know. The first step in preparing for the TACHS® is to assess your strengths and weaknesses. You may already have an idea of what you know and what you do not know, but evaluating yourself using our Self- Assessment modules for each of the three areas, Math, Writing and Quantitative skills, will clarify the details.

**Making a Study Schedule**

To make your study time most productive you will need to develop a study plan. The purpose of the plan is to organize all the bits of pieces of information in such a way that you will not feel overwhelmed. Rome was not built in a day, and learning everything you will need to know to pass the TACHS® is going to take time, too. Arranging the material you need to learn into manageable chunks is the best way to go. Each study session should make you feel as though you have succeeded in accomplishing your goal, and your goal is simply to learn what you planned to learn during that particular session. Try to organize the content in such a way that each study session builds upon previous ones. That way, you will retain the information, be better able to access it, and review the previous bits and pieces at the same time.

## Self-assessment

**The Best Study Tip!** The very best study tip is to start early! The longer you study regularly, the more you will retain and 'learn' the material. Studying for 1 hour per day for 20 days is far better than studying for 2 hours for 10 days.

### What don't you know?

The first step is to assess your strengths and weaknesses. You may already have an idea of where your weaknesses are, or you can take our Self-assessment modules for each of the content areas.

| Exam Component | Rate 1 to 5 |
|---|---|
| | |
| **Reading** | |
| | |
| **Logical Reasoning** | |
| | |
| **Reading Comprehension** | |
| | |
| **Mathematics** | |
| Basic Math & Arithmetic | |
| Algebra | |
| Geometry | |
| | |
| **Reading Comprehension** | |

# Making a Study Schedule

The key to making a study plan is to divide the material you need to learn into manageable sized pieces and learn it, while at the same time reviewing the material that you already know.

Using the table above, any scores of 3 or below, you need to spend time learning, going over and practicing this subject area. A score of 4 means you need to review the material, but you don't have to spend time re-learning. A score of 5 and you are OK with just an occasional review before the exam.
A score of 0 or 1 means you really need to work on this should allocate the most time and the highest priority.
Some students prefer a 5-day plan and others a 10-day plan. It also depends on how much time you have until the exam.

Here is an example of a 5-day plan based on an example from the table above:

**Reading:** 1- Study 1 hour everyday – review on last day
**Logical Reasoning:** 4 - Review every second day
**Geometry:** 2 - Study 1 hour first day – then ½ hour everyday
**Algebra:** 5 - Review for ½ hour every other day
**Reading Comp.:** 5 - Review for ½ hour every other day

Using this example, reading comprehension and algebra are good and only need occasional review. Geometry is good and needs 'some' review. Geometry needs a bit of work, Word Problems need a lot of work and Reading are very weak and need the most time. Based on this, here is a sample study plan:

| Day | Subject | Time |
|---|---|---|
| **Monday** | | |
| Study | Reading | 1 hour |
| Study | Word Problems | 1 hour |
| **½ hour break** | | |
| Study | Geometry | 1 hour |
| Review | Reading Comp. | ½ hour |
| **Tuesday** | | |
| Study | Reading | 1 hour |
| Study | Word Problems | ½ hour |
| **½ hour break** | | |
| Study | Geometry | ½ hour |
| Review | Algebra | ½ hour |
| Review | Reading Comp. | ½ hour |
| **Wednesday** | | |
| Study | Reading | 1 hour |
| Study | Word Problems | ½ hour |
| **½ hour break** | | |
| Study | Geometry | ½ hour |
| Review | Reading Comp. | ½ hour |
| **Thursday** | | |
| Study | Reading | ½ hour |
| Study | Word Problems | ½ hour |
| Review | Geometry | ½ hour |
| **½ hour break** | | |
| Review | Reading Comp. | ½ hour |
| Review | Algebra | ½ hour |
| **Friday** | | |
| Review | Reading | ½ hour |
| Review | Word Problems | ½ hour |
| Review | Geometry | ½ hour |
| **½ hour break** | | |
| Review | Algebra | ½ hour |
| Review | Reading Comp. | ½ hour |

Using this example, adapt the study plan to your own schedule. This schedule assumes 2 ½ - 3 hours available to study everyday for a 5 day period.

First, write out what you need to study and how much. Next figure out how many days you have before the test. Note, do NOT study on the last day before the test. On the last day before the test, you won't learn anything and will probably only confuse yourself.

Make a table with the days before the test and the number of hours you have available to study each day. We suggest working with 1 hour and ½ hour time slots.

Start filling in the blanks, with the subjects you need to study the most getting the most time and the most regular time slots (i.e. everyday) and the subjects that you know getting the least time (e.g. ½ hour every other day, or every 3rd day).

## Tips for making a schedule

**Once you make a schedule, stick with it!** Make your study sessions reasonable. If you make a study schedule and don't stick with it, you set yourself up for failure. Instead, schedule study sessions that are a bit shorter and set yourself up for success! Make sure your study sessions are do-able. Studying is hard work but after you pass, you can party and take a break!

**Schedule breaks.** Breaks are just as important as study time. Work out a rotation of studying and breaks that works for you.

**Build up study time.** If you find it hard to sit still and study for 1 hour straight-through, build up to it. Start with 20 minutes, and then take a break. Once you get used to 20-minute study sessions, increase the time to 30 minutes. Gradually work you way up to 1 hour.

**40 minutes to 1 hour is optimal.** Studying for longer than this is tiring and not productive. Studying for shorter isn't long enough to be productive.

**Studying Math.** Studying Math is different from studying other subjects because you use a different part of your brain. The best way to study math is to practice everyday. This will train your mind to think in a mathematical way. If you miss a day or days, the mathematical mind-set is gone, and you have to start all over again to build it up.

Study and practice math everyday for at least 5 days before the exam.

For more information, see our How to Study Guide at www.study-skills.ca.

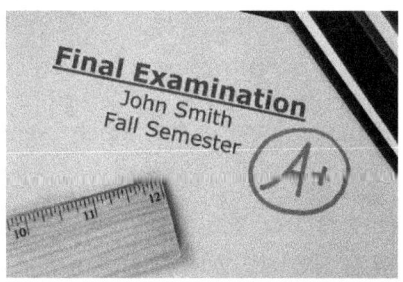

# Practice Test Questions Set 1

THE QUESTIONS BELOW ARE NOT THE SAME AS YOU WILL FIND ON THE TACHS - THAT WOULD BE TOO EASY! And nobody knows what the questions will be and they change all the time. Below are general questions that cover the same subject areas as the TACHS. So, while the format and exact wording of the questions may differ slightly, and change from year to year, if you can answer the questions below, you will have no problem with the TACHS.

For the best results, take these practice test questions as if it were the real exam. Set aside time when you will not be disturbed, and a location that is quiet and free of distractions. Read the instructions carefully, read each question carefully, and answer to the best of your ability.

Use the bubble answer sheets provided. When you have completed the practice questions, check your answer against the Answer Key and read the explanation provided.

Do not attempt more than one set of practice test questions in one day. After completing the first practice test, wait two or three days before attempting the second set of questions.

**Section I – Reading**
**Questions:** 50
**Time:** 35 minutes

**Section II - Language**
**Questions:** 50
**Time:** 30 minutes

**Section III – Mathematics**
**Questions:** 50
**Time:** 40 Minutes

**Section IV - Ability**
**Questions:** 40
**Time:** 30 Minutes

# Reading Answer Sheet

|    | A | B | C | D | E |     | A | B | C | D | E |
|----|---|---|---|---|---|-----|---|---|---|---|---|
| 1  | ○ | ○ | ○ | ○ | ○ | 26  | ○ | ○ | ○ | ○ | ○ |
| 2  | ○ | ○ | ○ | ○ | ○ | 27  | ○ | ○ | ○ | ○ | ○ |
| 3  | ○ | ○ | ○ | ○ | ○ | 28  | ○ | ○ | ○ | ○ | ○ |
| 4  | ○ | ○ | ○ | ○ | ○ | 29  | ○ | ○ | ○ | ○ | ○ |
| 5  | ○ | ○ | ○ | ○ | ○ | 30  | ○ | ○ | ○ | ○ | ○ |
| 6  | ○ | ○ | ○ | ○ | ○ | 31  | ○ | ○ | ○ | ○ | ○ |
| 7  | ○ | ○ | ○ | ○ | ○ | 32  | ○ | ○ | ○ | ○ | ○ |
| 8  | ○ | ○ | ○ | ○ | ○ | 33  | ○ | ○ | ○ | ○ | ○ |
| 9  | ○ | ○ | ○ | ○ | ○ | 34  | ○ | ○ | ○ | ○ | ○ |
| 10 | ○ | ○ | ○ | ○ | ○ | 35  | ○ | ○ | ○ | ○ | ○ |
| 11 | ○ | ○ | ○ | ○ | ○ | 36  | ○ | ○ | ○ | ○ | ○ |
| 12 | ○ | ○ | ○ | ○ | ○ | 37  | ○ | ○ | ○ | ○ | ○ |
| 13 | ○ | ○ | ○ | ○ | ○ | 38  | ○ | ○ | ○ | ○ | ○ |
| 14 | ○ | ○ | ○ | ○ | ○ | 39  | ○ | ○ | ○ | ○ | ○ |
| 15 | ○ | ○ | ○ | ○ | ○ | 40  | ○ | ○ | ○ | ○ | ○ |
| 16 | ○ | ○ | ○ | ○ | ○ | 41  | ○ | ○ | ○ | ○ | ○ |
| 17 | ○ | ○ | ○ | ○ | ○ | 42  | ○ | ○ | ○ | ○ | ○ |
| 18 | ○ | ○ | ○ | ○ | ○ | 43  | ○ | ○ | ○ | ○ | ○ |
| 19 | ○ | ○ | ○ | ○ | ○ | 44  | ○ | ○ | ○ | ○ | ○ |
| 20 | ○ | ○ | ○ | ○ | ○ | 45  | ○ | ○ | ○ | ○ | ○ |
| 21 | ○ | ○ | ○ | ○ | ○ | 46  | ○ | ○ | ○ | ○ | ○ |
| 22 | ○ | ○ | ○ | ○ | ○ | 47  | ○ | ○ | ○ | ○ | ○ |
| 23 | ○ | ○ | ○ | ○ | ○ | 48  | ○ | ○ | ○ | ○ | ○ |
| 24 | ○ | ○ | ○ | ○ | ○ | 49  | ○ | ○ | ○ | ○ | ○ |
| 25 | ○ | ○ | ○ | ○ | ○ | 50  | ○ | ○ | ○ | ○ | ○ |

## Language Answer Sheet

|   | A | B | C | D | E |   |   | A | B | C | D | E |
|---|---|---|---|---|---|---|---|---|---|---|---|---|
| 1 | ○ | ○ | ○ | ○ | ○ |   | 26 | ○ | ○ | ○ | ○ | ○ |
| 2 | ○ | ○ | ○ | ○ | ○ |   | 27 | ○ | ○ | ○ | ○ | ○ |
| 3 | ○ | ○ | ○ | ○ | ○ |   | 28 | ○ | ○ | ○ | ○ | ○ |
| 4 | ○ | ○ | ○ | ○ | ○ |   | 29 | ○ | ○ | ○ | ○ | ○ |
| 5 | ○ | ○ | ○ | ○ | ○ |   | 30 | ○ | ○ | ○ | ○ | ○ |
| 6 | ○ | ○ | ○ | ○ | ○ |   | 31 | ○ | ○ | ○ | ○ | ○ |
| 7 | ○ | ○ | ○ | ○ | ○ |   | 32 | ○ | ○ | ○ | ○ | ○ |
| 8 | ○ | ○ | ○ | ○ | ○ |   | 33 | ○ | ○ | ○ | ○ | ○ |
| 9 | ○ | ○ | ○ | ○ | ○ |   | 34 | ○ | ○ | ○ | ○ | ○ |
| 10 | ○ | ○ | ○ | ○ | ○ |   | 35 | ○ | ○ | ○ | ○ | ○ |
| 11 | ○ | ○ | ○ | ○ | ○ |   | 36 | ○ | ○ | ○ | ○ | ○ |
| 12 | ○ | ○ | ○ | ○ | ○ |   | 37 | ○ | ○ | ○ | ○ | ○ |
| 13 | ○ | ○ | ○ | ○ | ○ |   | 38 | ○ | ○ | ○ | ○ | ○ |
| 14 | ○ | ○ | ○ | ○ | ○ |   | 39 | ○ | ○ | ○ | ○ | ○ |
| 15 | ○ | ○ | ○ | ○ | ○ |   | 40 | ○ | ○ | ○ | ○ | ○ |
| 16 | ○ | ○ | ○ | ○ | ○ |   | 41 | ○ | ○ | ○ | ○ | ○ |
| 17 | ○ | ○ | ○ | ○ | ○ |   | 42 | ○ | ○ | ○ | ○ | ○ |
| 18 | ○ | ○ | ○ | ○ | ○ |   | 43 | ○ | ○ | ○ | ○ | ○ |
| 19 | ○ | ○ | ○ | ○ | ○ |   | 44 | ○ | ○ | ○ | ○ | ○ |
| 20 | ○ | ○ | ○ | ○ | ○ |   | 45 | ○ | ○ | ○ | ○ | ○ |
| 21 | ○ | ○ | ○ | ○ | ○ |   | 46 | ○ | ○ | ○ | ○ | ○ |
| 22 | ○ | ○ | ○ | ○ | ○ |   | 47 | ○ | ○ | ○ | ○ | ○ |
| 23 | ○ | ○ | ○ | ○ | ○ |   | 48 | ○ | ○ | ○ | ○ | ○ |
| 24 | ○ | ○ | ○ | ○ | ○ |   | 49 | ○ | ○ | ○ | ○ | ○ |
| 25 | ○ | ○ | ○ | ○ | ○ |   | 50 | ○ | ○ | ○ | ○ | ○ |

# Mathematics Answer Sheet

|    | A | B | C | D | E |    | A | B | C | D | E |
|----|---|---|---|---|---|----|---|---|---|---|---|
| 1  | ○ | ○ | ○ | ○ | ○ | 26 | ○ | ○ | ○ | ○ | ○ |
| 2  | ○ | ○ | ○ | ○ | ○ | 27 | ○ | ○ | ○ | ○ | ○ |
| 3  | ○ | ○ | ○ | ○ | ○ | 28 | ○ | ○ | ○ | ○ | ○ |
| 4  | ○ | ○ | ○ | ○ | ○ | 29 | ○ | ○ | ○ | ○ | ○ |
| 5  | ○ | ○ | ○ | ○ | ○ | 30 | ○ | ○ | ○ | ○ | ○ |
| 6  | ○ | ○ | ○ | ○ | ○ | 31 | ○ | ○ | ○ | ○ | ○ |
| 7  | ○ | ○ | ○ | ○ | ○ | 32 | ○ | ○ | ○ | ○ | ○ |
| 8  | ○ | ○ | ○ | ○ | ○ | 33 | ○ | ○ | ○ | ○ | ○ |
| 9  | ○ | ○ | ○ | ○ | ○ | 34 | ○ | ○ | ○ | ○ | ○ |
| 10 | ○ | ○ | ○ | ○ | ○ | 35 | ○ | ○ | ○ | ○ | ○ |
| 11 | ○ | ○ | ○ | ○ | ○ | 36 | ○ | ○ | ○ | ○ | ○ |
| 12 | ○ | ○ | ○ | ○ | ○ | 37 | ○ | ○ | ○ | ○ | ○ |
| 13 | ○ | ○ | ○ | ○ | ○ | 38 | ○ | ○ | ○ | ○ | ○ |
| 14 | ○ | ○ | ○ | ○ | ○ | 39 | ○ | ○ | ○ | ○ | ○ |
| 15 | ○ | ○ | ○ | ○ | ○ | 40 | ○ | ○ | ○ | ○ | ○ |
| 16 | ○ | ○ | ○ | ○ | ○ | 41 | ○ | ○ | ○ | ○ | ○ |
| 17 | ○ | ○ | ○ | ○ | ○ | 42 | ○ | ○ | ○ | ○ | ○ |
| 18 | ○ | ○ | ○ | ○ | ○ | 43 | ○ | ○ | ○ | ○ | ○ |
| 19 | ○ | ○ | ○ | ○ | ○ | 44 | ○ | ○ | ○ | ○ | ○ |
| 20 | ○ | ○ | ○ | ○ | ○ | 45 | ○ | ○ | ○ | ○ | ○ |
| 21 | ○ | ○ | ○ | ○ | ○ | 46 | ○ | ○ | ○ | ○ | ○ |
| 22 | ○ | ○ | ○ | ○ | ○ | 47 | ○ | ○ | ○ | ○ | ○ |
| 23 | ○ | ○ | ○ | ○ | ○ | 48 | ○ | ○ | ○ | ○ | ○ |
| 24 | ○ | ○ | ○ | ○ | ○ | 49 | ○ | ○ | ○ | ○ | ○ |
| 25 | ○ | ○ | ○ | ○ | ○ | 50 | ○ | ○ | ○ | ○ | ○ |

## Ability Answer Sheet

|    | A | B | C | D | E |    | A | B | C | D | E |
|----|---|---|---|---|---|----|---|---|---|---|---|
| 1  | ○ | ○ | ○ | ○ | ○ | 21 | ○ | ○ | ○ | ○ | ○ |
| 2  | ○ | ○ | ○ | ○ | ○ | 22 | ○ | ○ | ○ | ○ | ○ |
| 3  | ○ | ○ | ○ | ○ | ○ | 23 | ○ | ○ | ○ | ○ | ○ |
| 4  | ○ | ○ | ○ | ○ | ○ | 24 | ○ | ○ | ○ | ○ | ○ |
| 5  | ○ | ○ | ○ | ○ | ○ | 25 | ○ | ○ | ○ | ○ | ○ |
| 6  | ○ | ○ | ○ | ○ | ○ | 26 | ○ | ○ | ○ | ○ | ○ |
| 7  | ○ | ○ | ○ | ○ | ○ | 27 | ○ | ○ | ○ | ○ | ○ |
| 8  | ○ | ○ | ○ | ○ | ○ | 28 | ○ | ○ | ○ | ○ | ○ |
| 9  | ○ | ○ | ○ | ○ | ○ | 29 | ○ | ○ | ○ | ○ | ○ |
| 10 | ○ | ○ | ○ | ○ | ○ | 30 | ○ | ○ | ○ | ○ | ○ |
| 11 | ○ | ○ | ○ | ○ | ○ | 31 | ○ | ○ | ○ | ○ | ○ |
| 12 | ○ | ○ | ○ | ○ | ○ | 32 | ○ | ○ | ○ | ○ | ○ |
| 13 | ○ | ○ | ○ | ○ | ○ | 33 | ○ | ○ | ○ | ○ | ○ |
| 14 | ○ | ○ | ○ | ○ | ○ | 34 | ○ | ○ | ○ | ○ | ○ |
| 15 | ○ | ○ | ○ | ○ | ○ | 35 | ○ | ○ | ○ | ○ | ○ |
| 16 | ○ | ○ | ○ | ○ | ○ | 36 | ○ | ○ | ○ | ○ | ○ |
| 17 | ○ | ○ | ○ | ○ | ○ | 37 | ○ | ○ | ○ | ○ | ○ |
| 18 | ○ | ○ | ○ | ○ | ○ | 38 | ○ | ○ | ○ | ○ | ○ |
| 19 | ○ | ○ | ○ | ○ | ○ | 39 | ○ | ○ | ○ | ○ | ○ |
| 20 | ○ | ○ | ○ | ○ | ○ | 40 | ○ | ○ | ○ | ○ | ○ |

# Section I - Reading

# Part I - Vocabulary

**Directions:** Choose the word that is closest in meaning to the underlined word.

**1. The <u>cut</u> on her knee is bleeding.**

    a. Slice

    b. Chop

    c. Gash

    d. Bone

**2. Smoking can cause cancer. It is <u>hazardous</u> to one's health.**

    a. Safe

    b. Beneficial

    c. Important

    d. Dangerous

**3. The house has no lights on. It looks <u>dark</u>.**

    a. Shadowy

    b. Sad

    c. Bright

    d. Scary

**4. The judges will <u>determine</u> the winner of the contest.**

    a. Award

    b. Choose

    c. Congratulate

    d. Explain

**5. Please give us a <u>definite</u> answer to the question.**

    a. Unclear
    b. Wrong
    c. Clear
    d. Different

**6. I can't wait to try some of the <u>delectable</u> dishes served in the new restaurant.**

    a. Unique
    b. Expensive
    c. New
    d. Delicious

**7. Can you <u>describe</u> the character of Juliet in the play?**

    a. Report
    b. Portray
    c. Explain
    d. Draw

**8. The soldiers will <u>destroy</u> the camps of the rebels.**

    a. Ruin
    b. End
    c. Fix
    d. Conquer

**9. There is a big <u>difference</u> in the grades of Esther with that of Pete.**

    a. Complication
    b. Dissimilarity
    c. Minus
    d. Increase

**10. I can <u>attain</u> my goals in life if I study hard.**

    a. Finish
    b. Forget
    c. Effect
    d. Achieve

**11. The lecture was so <u>boring</u> everybody was starting to get sleepy.**

    a. Uninteresting
    b. Sensible
    c. Fast
    d. Exciting

**12. The <u>eager</u> crowd yelled and cheered for their favorite team during the basketball tournament.**

    a. Bored
    b. Uninterested
    c. Angry
    d. Enthusiastic

**13. The government is planning to <u>end</u> famine through mass food production.**

    a. Close
    b. Avoid
    c. Stop
    d. Start

**14. Children <u>enjoy</u> playing in the park with their playmates.**

    a. Dislike
    b. Delight in
    c. Spend
    d. Uninterested

**15. Can you <u>elaborate</u> on the reason behind your tardiness in class?**

　　a. Define
　　b. Correct
　　c. Explain
　　d. Interpret

**16. An evident or clear obvious truth.**

　　a. Truism
　　b. Catharsis
　　c. Libertine
　　d. Tractable

**17. Choose the best definition for: virago**

　　a. A loud domineering woman
　　b. A quiet woman
　　c. A load domineering Man
　　d. A quiet man

**18. When Joe broke his _____ in a skiing accident, his entire leg was in a cast.**

　　a. Ankle
　　b. Humerus
　　c. Wrist
　　d. Femur

**19. Select another word for the underlined word in the sentence below.**

At first I thought she was very rude and boorish, but when I talked to her again she was very **genteel**.

    a. Chivalrous

    b. Hilarious

    c. Civilized

    d. Governance

**20. Choose an adjective that means corrupted, impure.**

    a. Adulterate

    b. Harbor

    c. Infuriate

    d. Inculcate

# Part II - Reading Comprehension

**Directions:** Read each passage below carefully and then answer the questions that follow. Be careful to choose the best answer, given the four choices and only base your answer on the information given in the passage.

**Questions 21 – 24 refer to the following passage.**

**Passage 1 - The Life of Helen Keller**

Many people have heard of Helen Keller. She is famous because she was unable to see or hear, but learned to speak and read and went onto attend college and earn a degree. Her life is a very interesting story, one that she developed into an autobiography, which was then adapted into both a stage play and a movie. How did Helen Keller overcome her disabilities to become a famous woman? Read onto find out.

Helen Keller was not born blind and deaf. When she was a small baby, she had a very high fever for several days. As a result of her sudden illness, baby Helen lost her eyesight and her hearing. Because she was so young when she went deaf and blind, Helen Keller never had any recollection of being able to see or hear. Since she could not hear, she could not learn to talk. Since she could not see, it was difficult for her to move around. For the first six years of her life, her world was very still and dark.

Imagine what Helen's childhood was like. She could not hear her mother's voice. She could not see the beauty of her parent's farm. She could not recognize who was giving her a hug, or a bath or even where her bedroom was each night. More sad, she could not communicate with her parents in any way. She could not express her feelings or tell them the things she wanted. It must have been a very sad childhood.

When Helen was six years old, her parents hired her a teacher named Anne Sullivan. Anne was a young woman who was almost blind. However, she could hear and she could read Braille, so she was a perfect teacher for young Helen. At first, Anne had a very hard time teaching Helen anything. She described her first impression of Helen as a "wild thing, not a child." Helen did not like Anne at first either. She bit and hit Anne when Anne tried to teach her. However, the two of them eventually came to have a great deal of love and respect.

Anne taught Helen to hear by putting her hands on people's throats. She could feel the sounds that people made. In time, Helen learned to feel what people said. Next, Anne taught Helen to read Braille, which is a way that books are written for the blind. Finally, Anne taught Helen to talk. Although Helen did learn to talk, it was hard for anyone but Anne to understand her.

As Helen grew older, more and more people were amazed by her story. She went to college and wrote books about her life. She gave talks to the public, with Anne at her side, translating her words. Today, both Anne Sullivan and Helen Keller are famous women who are respected for their lives' work.

**21. Helen Keller could not see and hear and so, what was her biggest problem in childhood?**

    a. Inability to communicate

    b. Inability to walk

    c. Inability to play

    d. Inability to eat

**22. Helen learned to hear by feeling the vibrations people made when they spoke. What were these vibrations were felt through?**

    a. Mouth

    b. Throat

    c. Ears

    d. Lips

**23. From the passage, we can infer that Anne Sullivan was a patient teacher. We can infer this because**

    a. Helen hit and bit her and Anne still remained her teacher.

    b. Anne taught Helen to read only.

    c. Anne was hard of hearing too.

    d. Anne wanted to be a teacher.

**24. Helen Keller learned to speak but Anne translated her words when she spoke in public. The reason Helen needed a translator was because**

    a. Helen spoke another language.

    b. Helen's words were hard for people to understand.

    c. Helen spoke very quietly.

    d. Helen did not speak but only used sign language.

**Questions 25 – 27 refer to the following passage.**

**Passage 2 - Ways Characters Communicate in Theater**

Playwrights give their characters voices in a way that gives depth and added meaning to what happens on stage during their play. There are different types of speech in scripts that allow characters to talk with themselves, with other characters, and even with the audience.

It is very unique to theater that characters may talk "to themselves." When characters do this, the speech they give is called a soliloquy. Soliloquies are usually poetic, introspective, moving, and can tell audience members about the feelings, motivations, or suspicions of an individual character without that character having to reveal them to other characters on stage. "To be or not to be" is a famous soliloquy given by Hamlet as he considers difficult but important themes, such as life and death.

The most common type of communication in plays is when one character is speaking to another or a group of other characters. This is generally called dialogue, but can also be called monologue if one character speaks without being interrupted for a long time. It is not necessarily the most important type of communication, but it is the most common because the plot of the play cannot really progress without it.

Lastly, and most unique to theater (although it has been used somewhat in film) is when a character speaks directly to the audience. This is called an aside, and scripts usually specifically direct actors to do this. Asides are usually comical, an inside joke between the character and the audience, and very short. The actor will usually face the audience when delivering them, even if it's for a moment, so the audience can recognize this move as an aside.

All three of these types of communication are important to the art of theater, and have been perfected by famous playwrights like Shakespeare. Understanding these types of communication can help an audience member grasp what is artful about the script and action of a play.

**25. According to the passage, characters in plays communicate to**

    a. move the plot forward

    b. show the private thoughts and feelings of one character

    c. make the audience laugh

    d. add beauty and artistry to the play

**26. When Hamlet delivers "To be or not to be," he can most likely be described as**

    a. solitary

    b. thoughtful

    c. dramatic

    d. hopeless

**27. The author uses parentheses to punctuate "although it has been used somewhat in film,"**

    a. to show that films are less important

    b. instead of using commas so that the sentence is not interrupted

    c. because parenthesis help separate details that are not as important

    d. to show that films are not as artistic

**Questions 28 – 30 refer to the following passage.**

**Passage 3 - Low Blood Sugar**

As the name suggest, low blood sugar is low sugar levels in the bloodstream. This can occur when you have not eaten properly and undertake strenuous activity, or, when you are very hungry. When Low blood sugar occurs regularly and is ongoing, it is a medical condition called hypoglycemia. This condition can occur in diabetics and in healthy adults.

Causes of low blood sugar can include excessive alcohol consumption, metabolic problems, stomach surgery, pancreas, liver or kidneys problems, as well as a side-effect of some medications.

**Symptoms**

There are different symptoms depending on the severity of the case.

Mild hypoglycemia can lead to feelings of nausea and hunger. The patient may also feel nervous, jittery and have fast heart beats. Sweaty skin, clammy and cold skin are likely symptoms.
Moderate hypoglycemia can result in a short temper, confusion, nervousness, fear and blurring of vision. The patient may feel weak and unsteady.

Severe cases of hypoglycemia can lead to seizures, coma, fainting spells, nightmares, headaches, excessive sweats and severe tiredness.

**Diagnosis of low blood sugar**

A doctor can diagnosis this medical condition by asking the patient questions and testing blood and urine samples. Home testing kits are available for patients to monitor blood sugar levels. It is important to see a qualified doctor though. The doctor can administer tests to ensure that will safely rule out other medical conditions that could affect blood sugar levels.

**Treatment**

Quick treatments include drinking or eating foods and drinks with high sugar contents. Good examples include soda, fruit juice, hard candy and raisins. Glucose energy tablets can also help. Doctors may also recommend medications and well as changes in diet and exercise routine to treat chronic low blood sugar.

## 28. Based on the article, which of the following is true?

    a. Low blood sugar can happen to anyone.

    b. Low blood sugar only happens to diabetics.

    c. Low blood sugar can occur even.

    d. None of the statements are true.

## 29. Which of the following are the author's opinion?

    a. Quick treatments include drinking or eating foods and drinks with high sugar contents.

    b. None of the statements are opinions.

    c. This condition can occur in diabetics and also in healthy adults.

    d. There are different symptoms depending on the severity of the case

## 30. What is the author's purpose?

    a. To inform

    b. To persuade

    c. To entertain

    d. To analyze

## 31. Which of the following is not a detail?

    a. A doctor can diagnosis this medical condition by asking the patient questions and testing.

    b. A doctor will test blood and urine samples.

    c. Glucose energy tablets can also help.

    d. Home test kits monitor blood sugar levels.

    d. None of the above.

**Questions 32 – 35 refer to the following passage.**

**How To Get A Good Nights Sleep**

Sleep is just as essential for healthy living as water, air and food. Sleep allows the body to rest and replenish depleted energy levels. Sometimes we may for various reasons experience difficulty sleeping which has a serious effect on our health. Those who have prolonged sleeping problems are facing a serious medical condition and should see a qualified doctor when possible for help. Here is simple guide that can help you sleep better at night.

Try to create a natural pattern of waking up and sleeping around the same time everyday. This means avoiding going to bed too early and oversleeping past your usual wake up time. Going to bed and getting up at radically different times everyday confuses your body clock. Try to establish a natural rhythm as much as you can.

Exercises and a bit of physical activity can help you sleep better at night. If you are having problem sleeping, try to be as active as you can during the day. If you are tired from physical activity, falling asleep is a natural and easy process for your body. If you remain inactive during the day, you will find it harder to sleep properly at night. Try walking, jogging, swimming or simple stretches as you get close to your bed time.

Afternoon naps are great to refresh you during the day, but they may also keep you awake at night. If you feel sleepy during the day, get up, take a walk and get busy to keep from sleeping. Stretching is a good way to increase blood flow to the brain and keep you alert so that you don't sleep during the day. This will help you sleep better night.

>A warm bath or a glass of milk in the evening can help your body relax and prepare for sleep. A cold bath will wake you up and keep you up for several hours. Also avoid eating too late before bed.

**32. How would you describe this sentence?**

   a. A recommendation
   b. An opinion
   c. A fact
   d. A diagnosis

**33. Which of the following is an alternative title for this article?**

   a. Exercise and a good night's sleep
   b. Benefits of a good night's sleep
   c. Tips for a good night's sleep
   d. Lack of sleep is a serious medical condition

**34. Which of the following cannot be inferred from this article?**

   a. Biking is helpful for getting a good night's sleep
   b. Mental activity is helpful for getting a good night's sleep
   c. Eating bedtime snacks is not recommended
   d. Getting up at the same time is helpful for a good night's sleep

**35. What is a disadvantage of taking naps?**

   a. They may keep you awake.
   b. There are no disadvantages
   c. They may help you sleep better
   d. They may affect your diet

**Question 36 refers to the following Table of Contents.**

**Contents**

    Science Self-assessment 81
    Answer Key 91
    Science Tutorials 96
    Scientific Method 96
    Biology 99
    Heredity: Genes and Mutation 104
    Classification 108
    Ecology 110
    Chemistry 112
    Energy: Kinetic and Mechanical 126
    Energy: Work and Power 130
    Force: Newton's Three Laws 132

**36. Consider the table of contents above. What page would you find information about natural selection and adaptation?**

    a. 81
    b. 90
    c. 110
    d. 132

**Questions 37 – 39 refer to the following passage.**

**Passage 5 - Pearl Harbor**

A Day That Will Live in Infamy! Attack on Pearl Harbor
In 1941, the world was at war. The United States was trying very hard to keep itself out of the conflict. In Europe, the countries of Germany and Italy had formed an alliance to expand their land and territory. Germany had already taken over Poland, Denmark, and parts of France. They were heading next toward England and due to all the fighting in Europe, there were battles taking place as far south as North Africa, where the German and Italian armies were fighting the British.

This got even worse when the Asian nation of Japan formed an alliance with Germany and Italy. Together, the three countries called themselves, the AXIS. Now, the war was in the Pacific as well as in Europe and Northern Africa. A great deal of Americans felt that perhaps now was the time for the United States to join with its ally, Great Britain and stop the Axis from taking over more regions of the world.

In 1941, Franklin Roosevelt was President of the United States. His fear at the time was that Japan would try to take over many countries in Asia. He did not want to see that happen, so he moved some of the United States warships that had been stationed in San Diego, to the military base at Pearl Harbor, in Honolulu, Hawaii.

Japan quietly plotted their attack. They waited until the early hours of the morning on Sunday, December 7, 1941. Then, 350 Japanese war plans began to drop bombs on the U.S. ships at Pearl Harbor. The first bombs fell at 7:48 am and a mere 90 minutes later, the attack was over. Pearl Harbor was decimated. 8 battleships were damaged. Eleven ships were sunk and 300 U.S. planes were destroyed. Most devastating was the loss of life 2,400 U.S. military members was killed in the attack and 1, 282 were injured.

President Roosevelt addressed the country via the radio and said "Today is a day that will live in infamy." He asked Congress to declare war on Japan. War was declared on Japan on December 8th and on Germany and Italy on December 11th. The United States had entered World War Two.

**37. After reading the passage, what can we infer infamy means?**

    a. Famous

    b. Remembered in a good way

    c. Remembered in a bad way

    d. Easily forgotten

**38. What three countries formed the Axis?**

    a. Italy, England, Germany

    b. United States, England, Italy

    c. Germany, Japan, Italy

    d. Germany, Japan, United States

**39. What do you think was President Roosevelt's reason for moving warships to Pearl Harbor?**

    a. He feared Japan would bomb San Diego

    b. He knew Japan was going to attack Pearl Harbor

    c. He was planning to attack Japan

    d. He wanted to try and protect Asian countries from Japanese takeover

**40. Why do you think Japan chose a Sunday morning at 7:48 am for their attack?**

    a. They knew the military slept late

    b. There is a law against bombing countries on a Sunday

    c. They wanted the attack to catch people by surprise

    d. That was the only free time they had to attack.

**Questions 41 - 44 refer to the following recipe.**

**If You Have Allergies, You're Not Alone**

People who experience allergies might joke that their immune systems have let them down or are seriously lacking. Truthfully though, people who experience allergic reactions or allergy symptoms during certain times of the year have heightened immune systems that are, "better" than those of people who have perfectly healthy but less militant immune systems.

Still, when a person has an allergic reaction, they are having an adverse reaction to a substance that is considered normal to most people. Mild allergic reactions usually have symptoms like itching, runny nose, red eyes, or bumps or discoloration of the skin. More serious allergic reactions, such as those to animal and insect poisons or certain foods, may result in the closing of the throat, swelling of the eyes, low blood pressure, inability to breath, and can even be fatal.

Different treatments help different allergies, and which one a person uses depends on the nature and severity of the allergy. It is recommended to patients with severe allergies to take extra precautions, such as carrying an EpiPen, which treats anaphylactic shock and may prevent death, always in order for the remedy to be readily available and more effective. When an allergy is not so severe, treatments may be used just relieve a person of uncomfortable symptoms. Over the counter allergy medicines treat milder symptoms, and can be bought at any grocery store and used in moderation to help people with allergies live normally.

There are many tests available to assess whether a person has allergies or what they may be allergic to, and advances in these tests and the medicine used to treat patients continues to improve. Despite this fact, allergies still affect many people throughout the year or even every day. Medicines used to treat allergies have side effects of their own, and it is difficult to bring the body into balance with the use of medicine. Regardless, many of those who live with allergies are grateful for what is available and find it useful in maintaining their lifestyles.

**41. According to this passage, it can be understood that the word "militant" belongs in a group with the words:**

    a. sickly, ailing, faint

    b. strength, power, vigor

    c. active, fighting, warring

    d. worn, tired, breaking down

**42. The author says that "medicines used to treat allergies have side-effects of their own" to**

a. point out that doctors aren't very good at diagnosing and treating allergies

b. argue that because of the large number of people with allergies, a cure will never be found

c. explain that allergy medicines aren't cures and some compromise must be made

d. argue that more wholesome remedies should be researched and medicines banned

**43. It can be inferred that _____ recommend that some people with allergies carry medicine with them.**

a. the author

b. doctors

c. the makers of EpiPen

d. people with allergies

**44. The author has written this passage to**

a. inform readers on symptoms of allergies so people with allergies can get help

b. persuade readers to be proud of having allergies

c. inform readers on different remedies so people with allergies receive the right help

d. describe different types of allergies, their symptoms, and their remedies

**Questions 45 – 46 refer to the following email.**

SUBJECT: MEDICAL STAFF CHANGES

To all staff:

This email is to advise you of a paper on recommended medical staff changes has been posted to the Human Resources website.

The contents are of primary interest to medical staff, other staff may be interested in reading it, particularly those in medical support roles.

The paper deals with several major issues:

> 1. Improving our ability to attract top quality staff to the hospital, and retain our existing staff. These changes will make our position and departmental names internationally recognizable and comparable with North American and North Asian departments and positions.

> 2. Improving our ability to attract top quality staff by introducing greater flexibility in the departmental structure.

> 3. General comments on issues to be further discussed in relation to research staff.

The changes outlined in this paper are significant. I encourage you to read the document and send to me any comments you may have, so that it can be enhanced and improved.

Gordon Simms
Administrator,
Seven Oaks Regional Hospital

## 45. Are all hospital staff required to read the document posted to the
## Human Resources website?

> a. Yes all staff are required to read the document.
> b. No, reading the document is optional.
> c. Only medical staff are required to read the document.
> d. none of the above are correct.

**46. Have the changes to medical staff been made?**

    a. Yes, the changes have been made.
    b. No, the changes are only being discussed.
    c. Some of the changes have been made.
    d. None of the choices are correct.

**Questions 47 – 50 refer to the following passage.**

**When a Poet Longs to Mourn, He Writes an Elegy**

Poems are an expressive, especially emotional, form of writing. They have been present in literature virtually from the time civilizations invented the written word. Poets often portrayed as moody, secluded, and even troubled, but this is because poets are introspective and feel deeply about the current events and cultural norms they are surrounded with. Poets often produce the most telling literature, giving insight into the society and mind-set they come from. This can be done in many forms.

The oldest types of poems often include many stanzas, may or may not rhyme, and are more about telling a story than experimenting with language or words. The most common types of ancient poetry are epics, which are usually extremely long stories that follow a hero through his journey, or ellegies, which are often solemn in tone and used to mourn or lament something or someone. The Mesopotamians are often said to have invented the written word, and their literature is among the oldest in the world, including the epic poem titled "Epic of Gilgamesh." Similar in style and length to "Gilgamesh" is "Beowulf," an ellegy written in Old English and set in Scandinavia. These poems are often used by professors as the earliest examples of literature.

The importance of poetry was revived in the Renaissance. At this time, Europeans discovered the style and beauty of ancient Greek arts, and poetry was among those. Shakespeare is the most well-known poet of the time, and he used poetry not only to write poems but also to write plays for the theater. The most popular forms of poetry during the Renaissance included villanelles, (a nineteen-line poetic form) sonnets, as well as the epic. Poets during this time focused on style and form, and developed very specific rules and outlines for how an exceptional poem should be written.

As often happens in the arts, modern poets have rejected the constricting rules of Renaissance poets, and free form poems are much more popular. Some modern poems would read just like stories if they weren't arranged into lines and stanzas. It is difficult to tell which poems and poets will be the most important, because works of art often become more famous in hindsight, after the poet has died and society can look at itself without being in the moment. Modern poetry continues to develop, and will no doubt continue to change as values, thought, and writing continue to change.

Poems can be among the most enlightening and uplifting texts for a person to read if they are looking to connect with the past, connect with other people, or try to gain an understanding of what is happening in their time.

**47. In summary, the author has written this passage**

> a. as a foreword that will introduce a poem in a book or magazine
>
> b. because she loves poetry and wants more people to like it
>
> c. to give a brief history of poems
>
> d. to convince students to write poems

**48. The author organizes the paragraphs mainly by**

> a. moving chronologically, explaining which types of poetry were common in that time
>
> b. talking about new types of poems each paragraph and explaining them a little
>
> c. focusing on one poet or group of people and the poems they wrote
>
> d. explaining older types of poetry so she can talk about modern poetry

**49. The author's claim that poetry has been around "virtually from the time civilizations invented the written word" is supported by the detail that**

  a. Beowulf is written in Old English, which is not really in use any longer

  b. epic poems told stories about heroes

  c. the Renaissance poets tried to copy Greek poets

  d. the Mesopotamians are credited with both inventing the word and writing "Epic of Gilgamesh"

**50. According to the passage, it can be understood that the word "telling" means**

  a. speaking

  b. significant

  c. soothing

  d. wordy

# Section II - Language
# Part I - English

**1. Choose the sentence with the correct grammar.**

  a. Don would never have thought of that book, but you could have reminded him.

  b. Don would never of thought of that book, but you could have reminded him.

  c. Don would never have thought of that book, but you could of have reminded him.

  d. Don would never of thought of that book, but you could of reminded him.

## 2. Choose the correct sentence.

a. The boy and girl are related.
b. The boy and girl is related.
c. The boy and girl was related.
d. None of the above.

## 3. Choose the sentence with the correct grammar.

a. There was scarcely no food in the pantry, because nobody ate at home.
b. There was scarcely any food in the pantry, because nobody ate at home.
c. There was scarcely any food in the pantry, because not nobody ate at home.
d. There was scarcely no food in the pantry, because not nobody ate at home.

## 4. Choose the sentence with the correct grammar.

a. Its important for you to know its official name; its called the Confederate Museum.
b. It's important for you to know it's official name; it's called the Confederate Museum.
c. It's important for you to know its official name; it's called the Confederate Museum.
d. Its important for you to know it's official name; it's called the Confederate Museum.

## 5. Choose the sentence with the correct grammar.

a. The man as well as his son has arrived.
b. The man as well as his son have arrived.
c. Both of the above.
d. None of the above.

**6. Thomas Edison _____ since he invented the light bulb, television, motion pictures, and phonograph.**

   a. has always been known as the greatest inventor

   b. was always been known as the greatest inventor

   c. must have had been always known as the greatest inventor

   d. will had been known as the greatest inventor

**7. The weatherman on Channel 6 said that this has been the**

   a. most hotter summer on record.

   b. most hottest summer on record.

   c. hottest summer on record.

   d. hotter summer on record.

**8. Although Joe is tall for his age, his brother Elliot is _____ of the two.**

   a. the tallest

   b. more tallest

   c. the tall

   d. the taller

**9. When KISS came to town, all of the tickets _____ before I could buy one.**

   a. will be sold out

   b. had been sold out

   c. were being sold out

   d. was sold out

**10. The rules of most sports _____ more complicated than we often realize.**

    a. are

    b. is

    c. was

    d. has been


**11. _____ won first place in the Western Division?**

    a. Who

    b. Whom

    c. Which

    d. What


**12. There are now several ways to listen to music, including radio, CDs, and Mp3 files _____ you can download onto an MP3 player.**

    a. on which

    b. who

    c. whom

    d. which


**13. Choose the sentence with the correct grammar.**

    a. Each of them have to be given a ticket.

    b. Each of them is to be given a ticket.

    c. Each of them are to be given a ticket.

    d. None of the above.

**14. Choose the correct spelling.**

a. maintainance
b. maintenace
c. maintanance
d. maintenance

**15. Choose the correct spelling.**

a. humoros
b. humouros
c. humorous
d. humorus

**16. Choose the correct spelling.**

a. mathematics
b. mathmatics
c. matematics
d. mathamatics

**17. Choose the sentence below with the correct punctuation.**

a. Ted and Janice, who had been friends for years, went on vacation together every summer.

b. Ted and Janice, who had been friends for years, went on vacation together, every summer.

c. Ted, and Janice who had been friends for years, went on vacation together every summer.

d. Ted and Janice who had been friends for years went on vacation together every summer.

**18. Choose the sentence with the correct capitalization.**

a. The Sahara Desert is found in the northern part of Africa.

b. The Sahara Desert is found in the Northern part of Africa.

c. The Sahara desert is found in the northern part of Africa.

d. The Sahara desert is found in the Northern part of Africa.

**19. She went with him to the dance.**

**What is the subject of this sentence?**

a. She
b. Dance
c. Him
d. With

**20. She studied long and hard and her marks showed it.**

**What is the predicate of this sentence?**

a. Studied long and hard
b. Marks showed it
c. Showed it
d. None of the above

**21. What is on the test?**

**What type of sentence is this?**

a. Imperative
b. Interrogative
c. Exclamatory
d. Declarative

**22. The aquarium featured brightly-colored tropical fish that came from the tropics.**

**What part of this sentence is redundant?**

    a. Brightly-colored

    b. Tropical fish

    c. That came from the tropics

    d. Aquarium

**23. Choose the correct sentence.**

    a. Historians have been guessing the doctor was a woman for more than 100 years.

    b. Historians have been guessing for more than 100 years the doctor was a woman.

    c. Historians guessed the doctor was a woman for more than 100 years.

    d. None of the above.

**24. Choose the correct sentence.**

    a. None of us want to go to the party not even, if there will be live music.

    b. None of us want to go to the party, not even if there will be live music.

    c. None of us want to go to the party not even if there will be live music.

    d. None of us want to go to the party; not even if there will be live music.

**25. Choose the correct sentence.**

    a. I own two dogs, a cat named Jeffrey, and Henry, the goldfish.

    b. I own two dogs  a cat, named Jeffrey, and Henry, the goldfish.

    c. I own two dogs, a cat named Jeffrey; and Henry, the goldfish.

    d. I own two dogs, a cat, named Jeffrey and Henry, the goldfish.

**26. Choose the correct sentence.**

a. During the years he was President, the country fought two wars.

b. During the years he was president, the country fought two wars.

c. During the years he was president, the Country fought two wars.

d. During the years he was President, the Country fought two wars.

**27. Alice <u>jumped</u> when she saw the rabbit.**

**What part of speech is the underlined word?**

a. Noun

b. Verb

c. Adjective

d. Adverb

**28. Which of the following sentences contains a redundant phrase?**

a. I will be leaving shortly.

b. I think the situation calls for a direct confrontation.

c. The fish swam upstream with great difficulty.

d. None of the above.

**Directions: For each of the questions below, choose the word with the meaning best suited to the sentence based on the context.**

**29. Paul's rose bushes were being destroyed by Japanese beetles, so he invested in a good _____.**

a. Fungicide

b. Fertilizer

c. Sprinkler

d. Pesticide

**30. Because of a pituitary dysfunction, Karl lacked the necessary _____ to grow as tall as his father.**

a. Glands

b. Hormones

c. Vitamins

d. Testosterone

# Part II - Paragraphs

## Curiosity's Mission

Mankind's thirst for knowledge about ourselves and the universe has always been insatiable, making curiosity a driving force for human advances through history. [1] Not only that, human curiosity and creativity have created countless works of fiction that speculate about future discoveries. [2]

Our neighboring planet Mars, for example, has long led scientists and writers to generate stories about living on the Red Planet. [3] Serious endeavors in science and technology are motivated by our never-ending questions. [4] So far, NASA has carried out several exploratory missions to Mars and the rover robot Curiosity is the latest and most sophisticated. [5]

Curiosity was launched in late November 2011 from Cape Canaveral Air Force Station in Florida. [6] It successfully landed on Mars on August 6, 2012 searching for evidence of life. [7] The car sized robot, weighing about a ton, is equipped with all the technical capacities to carry out its mission to explore our neighbor for biological, geological and geochemical traces of life. [8] It will also test the Martian soil and surface to collect data about its planetary evolution and surface radiation. [9]

Curiosity has been engineered with cutting-edge technologies worth over 2.5 billion US dollars. [10] The most incredible component of the rover is the on-board science lab. [11] Apart from that, it consists of a communications system that allows transmission of commands to the rover from the control centre at NASA, enabling direct control of the robot's activities on the surface of the Red Planet. [12] The Curiosity rover has a number of mounted cameras which assists navigation, as well as capturing images from the Martian surface and transmitting them back to Earth. [13]

**1. How would you re-write sentence 1?**

    a. No changes

    b. Mankind's thirst for knowledge has always been insatiable, making curiosity a driving factor for human advances through history.

    c. Mankind's thirst for knowledge is insatiable, making curiosity a driving factor for human advances through history.

    d. Humankind's thirst for knowledge is insatiable, making curiosity a driving force in advances throughout history.

**2. Which sentence in the third paragraph is least relevant to the main idea of the third paragraph?**

    a. 6
    b. 8
    c. 9
    d. 10

**3. Which of the following changes would focus attention on the main idea of the last paragraph?**

a. To achieve its goals, Curiosity has been engineered with cutting-edge technologies worth over 2.5 billion US dollars.

b. Because a lot of funding was available for this project, Curiosity has been engineered with cutting-edge technologies worth over 2.5 billion US dollars.

c. As there is no guarantee that it will succeed in its mission, Curiosity has been engineered with cutting-edge technologies worth over 2.5 billion US dollars.

d. NASA's scientific data is so reliable that, being assured of no risk of failure in the mission, Curiosity has been engineered with cutting-edge technologies worth over 2.5 billion US dollars.

**4. Which of the following is/are needed in sentence 5?**

a. So far, "NASA" has carried out several exploration missions to Mars and the rover robot Curiosity is the latest and most sophisticated of all.

b. So far, NASA has carried out several exploratory missions to Mars and the rover robot Curiosity is the latest and most sophisticated of all.

c. So far, NASA has carried out several exploration missions to Mars and the rover robot -Curiosity- is the latest and most sophisticated of all.

d. So far, NASA has carried out several exploratory missions to Mars and the rover robot "Curiosity" is the latest and most sophisticated of all.

## Green Energy from Olive Oil

The debate over developing sustainable energy sources have been very active in the past two decades. [1] With continued concern over global climate change, environmentalists are urging governments for lowering their dependence on fossil fuels in order for ensuring reduced carbon emission into the atmosphere. [2] Consequently, governments worldwide are turning their attention to the search for non-emissive sources of energy. [3] Renewable substitutes under extensive research are solar power, wind, geothermal energy and harnessing energy from ocean waves. [4]

While the search for environment friendly energy sources is already under way, developing these alternatives at a reasonable cost is a major challenge. [5] No cost-effective replacement for fossil fuels has yet been found. [6] However, recent years have seen remarkable progress in the field of solar energy. [7] Ted Sargent, a Professor at University of Toronto, Canada, has discovered that olive oil has the capacity to capture solar radiation and emit electrons resulting in an electric current. [8] This is a major discovery in the solar power generation industry as it offers a cheap source of harnessing the Sun's energy. [9]

Oleic acid, the main ingredient of olive oil, absorbs infrared radiation is the major component of the Sun's radiation reaching the Earth. [10] The discovery is significant because so far, no attempt has been made to use the abundant infrared radiation we receive throughout the year. [11] Capturing this heat wave radiation, along with the photons that are present in sunlight, increases the efficiency of thc solar cells that are already being manufactured commercially. [12] And to make it possible, Professor Sargent has developed a new kind of solar cell called "quantum dots," tiny cells made from gels of tin, bismuth, lead, sulphur and selenium mixed with extra pure olive oil. [13] The resulting ink-like crystal absorbs both photons and infrared radiation and has the capacity to transmit electrons and produce a current. [14]

This new method of capturing the Sun's energy is considered a breakthrough in the solar power industry as it offers cheaper alternatives to the existing use of silicon crystals which are costly to manufacture. [15] And although the invention is yet to prove its efficiency, a lot of funding has already been dedicated to further research. [16]

**5. What sentence from the passage is an example of a sentence fragment?**

    a. 6
    b. 10
    c. 11
    d. 13

**6. Which of the following sentences should be deleted to reduce redundancy?**

    a. 5
    b. 6
    c. 9
    d. 15

**7. Which of the following changes are needed in sentence 10?**

    a. Oleic acid, the main ingredient of olive oil, absorbs infrared radiation is the major component of the Sun's radiation reaching the Earth.

    b. Oleic acid, the main ingredient of olive oil, absorbs infrared radiation, which is the major component of the Sun's radiation reaching the Earth.

    c. Oleic acid, the main ingredient of olive oil absorbs infrared radiation that is the major component of the Sun's radiation reaching the Earth.

    d. Oleic acid, the main ingredient of olive oil, absorbs infrared radiation what is the major component of the Sun's radiation reaching the Earth.

## 8. Which of the following changes are needed in sentence 2?

a. With continued concern over global climate change, environmentalists are urging governments to lowering their dependence on fossil fuels to ensuring reduced carbon emission into the atmosphere.

b. With continued concern over global climate change, environmentalists are urging governments lower their dependence on fossil fuels in order for ensuring reduced carbon emission into the atmosphere.

c. With continued concern over global climate change, environmentalists are urging governments to lower their dependence on fossil fuels in order for ensuring reduced carbon emission into the atmosphere.

d. With continued concern over global climate change, environmentalists are urging governments to lower their dependence on fossil fuels to ensure reduced carbon emission into the atmosphere.

# Hunting Lost Cities from Space

Satellite imaging has become widespread with improvements in telecommunication over the past two decades. [1] Communication satellites in orbit around the Earth have enabled large-scale mapping of the planet's surface which has become freely available thanks to technology giants like Google. [2] Satellite mapping has opened up new possibilities in diverse fields of science and technology. [3]

The key feature of the new tool, according to Professor Sarah Parcak, who discovered many cities, temples and pyramids covered under sands and sediment; is that it offers a wider perspective in size and scale of the location under study. [4] Along with the visual information that the satellite images provide, numerous details about the sites can be obtained from infrared (IR) and gravitational field images. [5] This information, coupled with conventional on-site procedures, are vital for archeology. [6]

IR data collected from satellite imaging provide clues about the activities of humans living in the contemporary times of their civilizations- including their agriculture, vegetation, structures, habitation roads and much more. [7] This type of information is derived from IR imagery which detects IR radiation present in sunlight as it is reflected by the Earth. [8] Different points in a civilization reflect IR radiation in different proportions, revealing the contrast between different areas and provide detailed insight about the causes of these differing heat signatures. [9]

**9. Which of the following changes in sentence 6 would focus attention on the main idea of the second paragraph?**

a. These information, along with a supply of some heavy machinery, will help the excavation of every archeological site accomplished within a short period of time.

b. This information, coupled with conventional on-site procedures, help archeologists plan their excavation carefully and efficiently.

c. Such details are valuable records of ancient history and are essential assets of any civilization.

d. Such details, unfortunately, are available to archeological firms who are willing to invest a lot of money on putting satellites into orbit.

**10. Which of the following sentences should be modified to reduce redundancy?**

a. 7
b. 8
c. 9
d. 10

# Section III – Math

**1. Simplify 2 1/3 ÷ 1 2/5**

    a. 1 2/5
    b. 1 2/3
    c. 1 1/7
    d. 2 2/5

**2. 2/3 x 1 4/7 x 5 1/4**

    a. 3 1/4
    b. 5 1/2
    c. 6 2/3
    d. 4 2/5

**3. Simplify 4 1/5 ÷ 2 1/3**

    a. 1 4/5
    b. 2 1/4
    c. 1 3/7
    d. 2 1/4

**4. 10/3 x 2 1/4 x 3 1/5**

    a. 1 3/4
    b. 24
    c. 7 2/7
    d. 5 1/5

**5. Simplify 3 1/9 ÷ 2 2/3**

    a. 2 1/5
    b. 2 3/4
    c. 1 1/6
    d. 1 1/4

**6. What is -9 + (+6) – (-2)**

    a. -3
    b. -1
    c. 5
    d. -5

**7. Smith and Simon are playing a card game. Smith will win if a card drawn from a deck of 52 is either a 7 or a diamond, and Simon will win if the drawn card is an even number. Which statement is more likely to be correct?**

    a. Simon will win more games.

    b. Smith will win more games.

    c. They have same winning probability.

    d. A decision cannot be made from the provided data.

**8. By practicing, a typist increases his typing speed by 2 words per minute daily. If his current typing speed is 18 words per minute and he practice 3 hours a day, then how many hours will he need to practice to attain 40 words per minute?**

    a. 27
    b. 30
    c. 33
    d. 36

**9. If the speed of a train is 72 kilometers per hour, what distance will it cover in 12 seconds?**

    a. 200 m
    b. 220 m
    c. 240 m
    d. 260 m

10. In a class of 83 students, 72 are present. What percent of the students are absent? Provide answer up to two significant digits.

   a. 12
   b. 13
   c. 14
   d. 15


11. A driver traveled from city A to city B in 1 hour and 13 minutes. On the way, he had to stop at 5 traffic signals, with an average time of 80 seconds. If the distance between the cities is 65 kilometers then what was the average driving speed?

   a. 56.42
   b. 58.77
   c. 60.34
   d. 63.25


12. Mr. Micheal runs a factory. His total assets are $256,800 that consists of a building worth $80,500, machinery worth $125.000 and $51,300 cash. After one year what will be the value of his total assets if he has additional cash of $75,600 and the value of his building has increased by 10% per year, and his machinery depreciated by 20% per year?

   a. $24,3450
   b. $25,2450
   c. $26,4150
   d. $27,2350

13. Martin earns $25,000 as basic pay, $500 rent and $860 for medical insurance. He spends 40% of his total earning on food and clothing, 10% on children's education and pays $800 for utility bills. What percent of his earning he is saving?

   a. 54%
   b. 50%
   c. 47%
   d. 44%

14. Prize money of $1,050 is to be shared among top three contestants in ratio of 7:5:3 as 1st, 2nd and 3rd prizes respectively. How much more money will the 1st prize contestant receive than the 3rd prize contestant?

   a. $210
   b. $280
   c. $350
   d. $490

15. The manager of a weaving factory estimates that if 10 machines run on 100% efficiency for 8 hours, they will produce 1450 meters of cloth. Due to some technical problems, 4 machines run of 95% efficiency and the remaining 6 at 90% efficiency. How many meters of cloth can these machines will produce in 8 hours?

   a. 1479 meters
   b. 1310 meters
   c. 1334 meters
   d. 1285 meters

16. A car covers a distance in 3.5 hours at an average speed of 60 km/hr. How much time in hours will a motorbike take to cover this distance at an average speed of 40km/hr?

    a. 4.5
    b. 4.75
    c. 5
    d. 5.25

17. A grandfather is 8 times older than his grandson is now. After 6 years, he will be 5 times older than his grandson will. How old is the grandfather now?

    a. 48
    b. 56
    c. 64
    d. 72

18. Solve for n. 5n + (19 − 2)) = 67.

    a. 21
    b. 10
    c. 15
    d. 7

19. A boy is given 2 apples while his sister is given 8 oranges. What is the ratio between his apples and her oranges?

    a. 1:2
    b. 2:4
    c. 1:4
    d. 2:1

20. A box contains 7 black pencils and 28 blue ones. What is the ratio between the black and blue pens?

    a. 1:4
    b. 2:7
    c. 1:8
    d. 1:9

21. If X + (32 + 356) = 920. What is x?

    a. 450
    b. 388
    c. 532
    d. 623

22. A boy buys 10 candies. The packet contains 3 green candies, 12 red and 9 blue candies. What is the ratio the green, red and blue sweets?

    a. 1:3:4
    b. 1:4:3
    c. 2:3:1
    d. 1:5:4

23. Solve for x. (12 x 12)/x = 12

    a. 12
    b. 13
    c. 8
    d. 14

24. Solve for A. A − (34 x 2) = 18.

    a. 86
    b. 78
    c. 50
    d. 73

**25. Solve for X.  X% of 120 = 30.**

    a. 15
    b. 12
    c. 4
    d. 25

**26. Solve for X. X * 25% of 100 = 76.**

    a. 5
    b. 3
    c. 21
    d. 13

**27. Solve for X.  X% of 250 = 50.**

    a. 30
    b. 35
    c. 25
    d. 20

**28. What is the least common multiple of 4 and 3?**

    a. 24
    b. 6
    c. 16
    d. 12

**29. What is the ratio between 2 gold coins, 6 silver coins and 12 bronze coins?**

    a. 2:3:4
    b. 1:2:4
    c. 1:3:6
    d. 2:3:4

**30. What is the least common multiple of 8 and 12?**

    a. 24
    b. 36
    c. 12
    d. 8

**31. Solve for x. -7 + 3x = 20.**

    a. 7
    b. 5
    c. 4
    d. 9

**32. What is the least common multiple of 2 and 3?**

    a. 2
    b. 4
    c. 6
    d. 3

**33. Solve for c, when 124 = 12c - 20.**

    a. 6
    b. 12
    c. 10
    d. 15

**34. Simplify 3 8/9 + 5 5/6.**

    a. 8 13/15
    b. 8 3/9
    c. 9 13/18
    d. 8 12/18

**35. Simplify 7 4/5 + 2 2/5.**

   a. 5 3/5
   b. 5 1/5
   c. 4 2/5
   d. 5 2/5

**36. Translate the following into an equation: three plus a number times 7 equals 42.**

   a. 7(3 + X) = 42
   b. 3(X + 7) = 42
   c. 3X + 7 = 42
   d. (3 + 7)X = 42

**37. Estimate 5205 / 25**

   a. 108
   b. 308
   c. 208
   d. 408

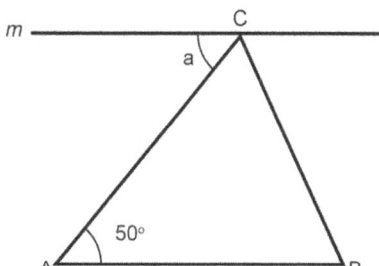

**Note:** figure not drawn to scale

**38. If the line m is parallel to the side AB of △ABC, what is angle a?**

    a. 130°
    b. 25°
    c. 65°
    d. 50°

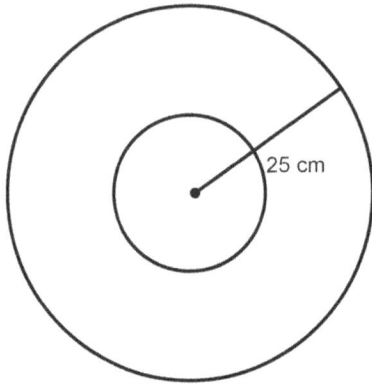

**Note:** figure not drawn to scale

**39. What is the distance travelled by the wheel above, when it makes 175 revolutions?**

    a. 87.5 π m
    b. 875 π m
    c. 8.75 π m
    d. 8750 π m

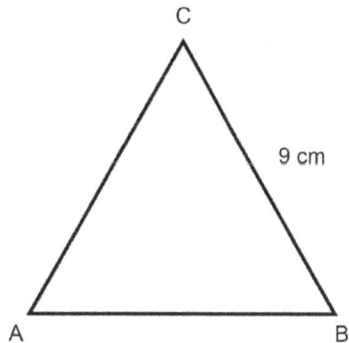

**Note:** figure not drawn to scale

## 40. What is the perimeter of the equilateral △ABC above?

    a. 18 cm
    b. 12 cm
    c. 27 cm
    d. 15 cm

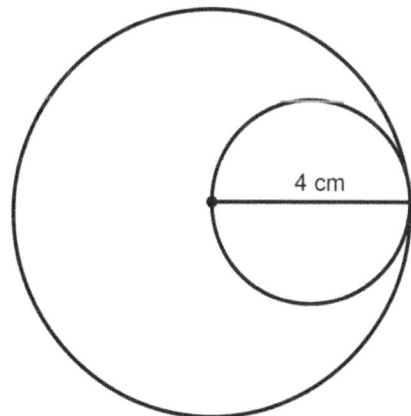

**Note:** figure not drawn to scale

**41.** Assuming the diameter of the small circle is the radius of the larger circle, what is (area of large circle) - (area of small circle) in the figure above?

   a. 8 π cm²
   b. 10 π cm²
   c. 12 π cm²
   d. 16 π cm²

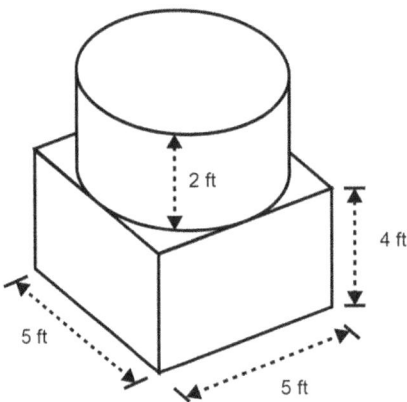

Note: figure not drawn to scale

**42.** What is the approximate total volume of the above solid?

   a. 120 ft³
   b. 100 ft³
   c. 140 ft³
   d. 160 ft³

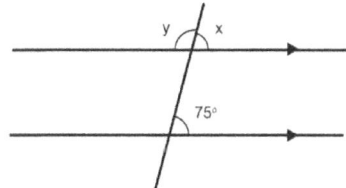

**43. What is the value of the angle y?**

   a. 25°
   b. 15°
   c. 30°
   d. 105°

**44. In a local election at polling station A, 945 voters cast their vote out of 1270 registered voters. At polling station B, 860 cast their vote out of 1050 registered voters and at station C, 1210 cast their vote out of 1440 registered voters. What is the total turnout including all three polling stations?**

   a. 70%
   b. 74%
   c. 76%
   d. 80%

**45. 3a + 4b x d =? When A = 2, b = 4 and d = 8.**

   a. 40
   b. 90
   c. 80
   d. 65

**46.** $4^2 \times 4^7 =$

    a. $16^{-5}$

    b. $4^9$

    c. $16^{11}$

    d. $4^{-5}$

**47.** $10^{65} \div 10^{13}$

    a. $10^{52}$

    b. $10^{78}$

    c. $100^{62}$

    d. $100^{78}$

**48. Consider the following population growth chart.**

| Country | Population 2000 | Population 2005 |
| --- | --- | --- |
| Japan | 122,251,000 | 128,057,000 |
| China | 1,145,195,000 | 1,341,335,000 |
| United States | 253,339,000 | 310,384,000 |
| Indonesia | 184,346,000 | 239,871,000 |

**What country is growing the fastest?**

    a. Japan

    b. China

    c. United States

    d. Indonesia

**49. What is the smallest value?**

a. 0.4 portion of 200
b. 50% of 100
c. 0.06 portion of 2000
d. 2% of 1000

**50. What number multiplied by 5 is 10 less than 52?**

a. 8.4
b. 10.24
c. 20
d. 22.5

## Section IV - Ability

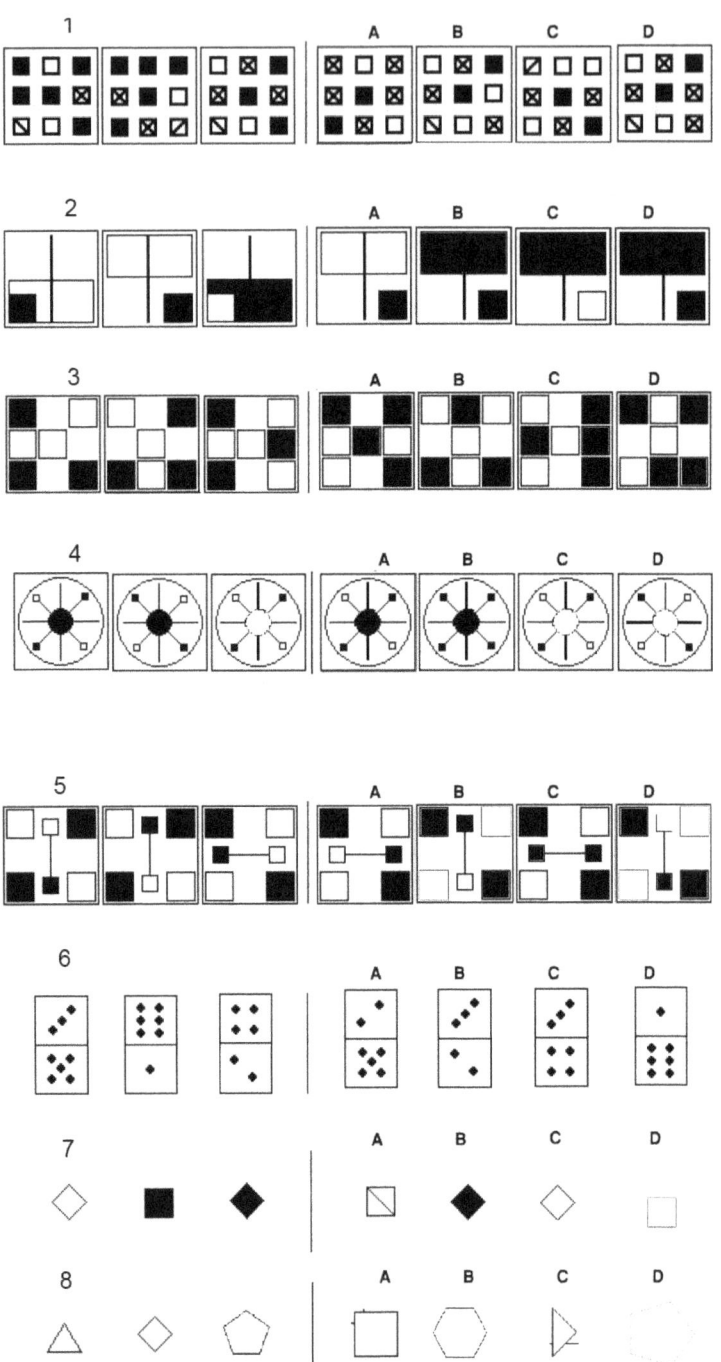

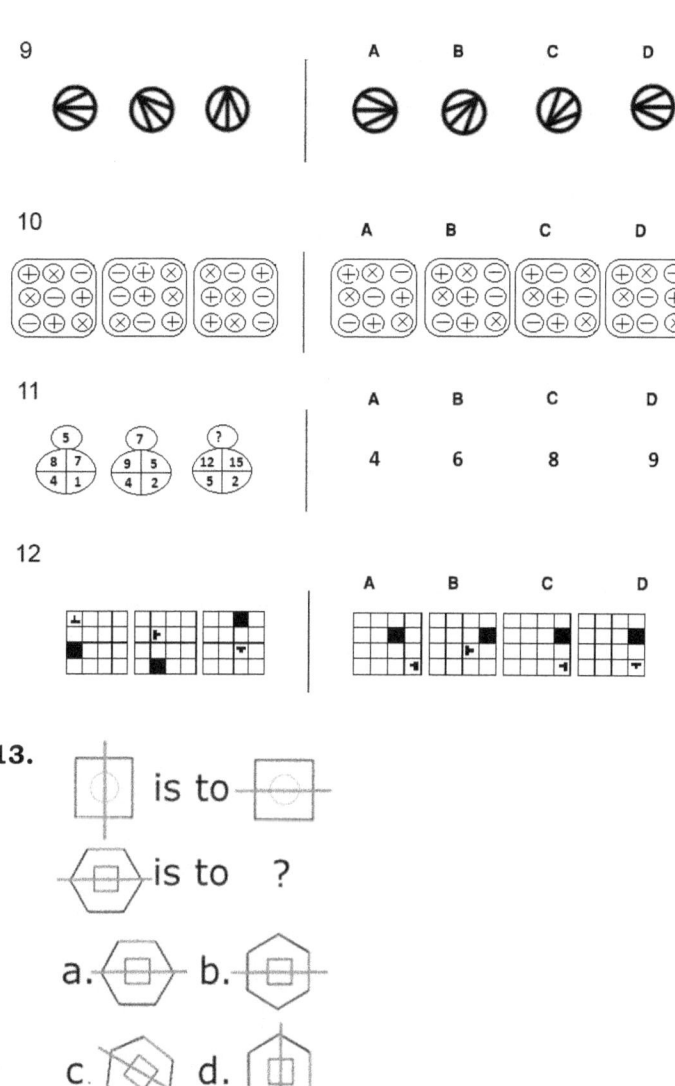

**14.**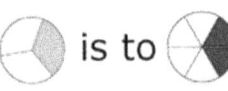

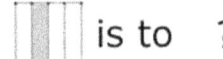

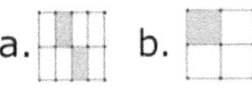

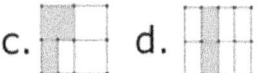

**15.**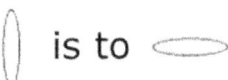

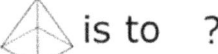

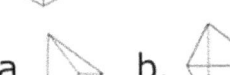

**16.**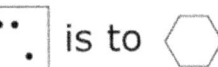

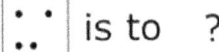

**17.**

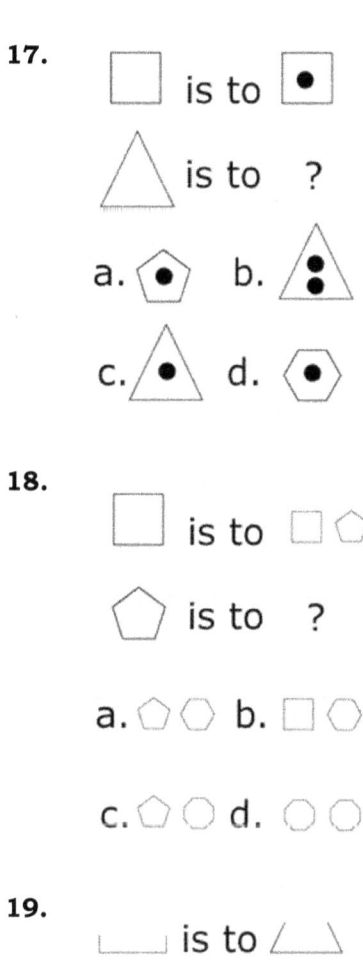

**18.**

☐ is to ☐⬠

⬠ is to ?

a. ⬠◯   b. ☐⬡

c. ⬠◯   d. ◯◯

**19.**

▭ is to ◺

⏌⎿ is to ?

a. ⌒⌐   b. ◁◺

c. ⎵   d. ◺

**20.**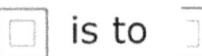

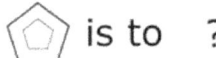

a. )    b. ⟩

c. ⟩    d. ]

**21.** is to

is to ?

a. )    b. ⟩

c. )    d. ]

**22.**

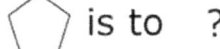

a. △    b. |||

c. ⊞    d.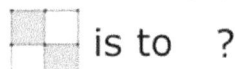

23.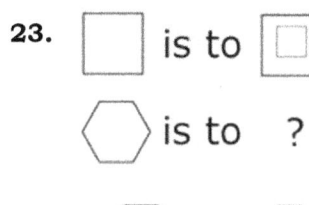

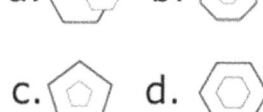

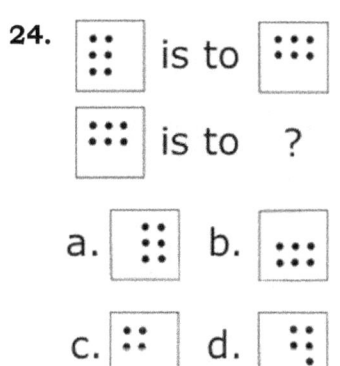

24.

25. **When folded, which shape is possible?**

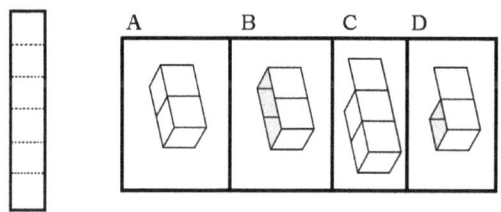

**26. When folded, what pattern is possible?**

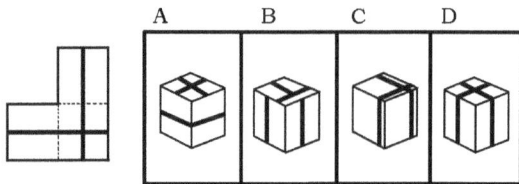

**27. When folded into a loop, what will the strip of paper look like?**

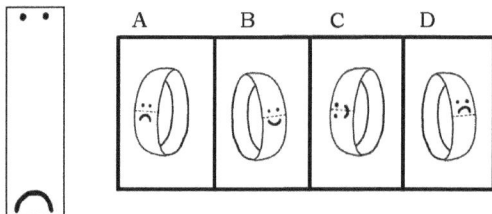

**28. Which of the choices is the same pattern at a different angle?**

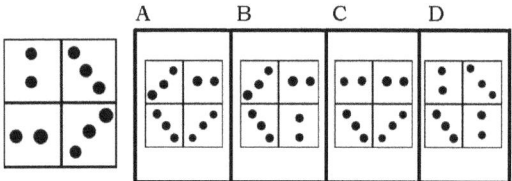

**29. When folded along the dotted lines, which shape will you get?**

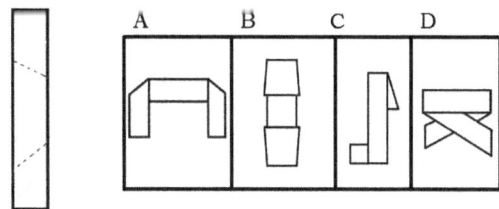

**30. When folded, what pattern is possible?**

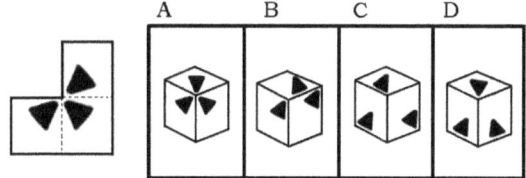

**31. When folded into a loop, what will the strip of paper look like?**

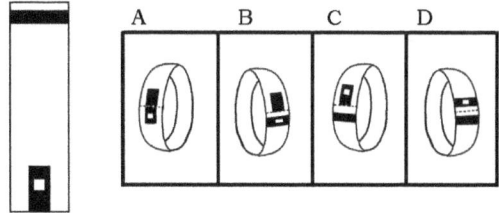

**32. Which of the choices is the same pattern at a different angle?**

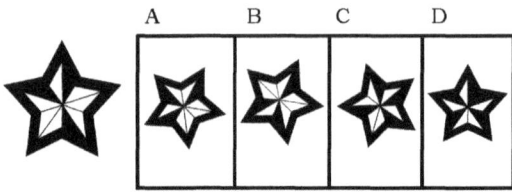

**33. When folded along the dotted line, which shape will you get?**

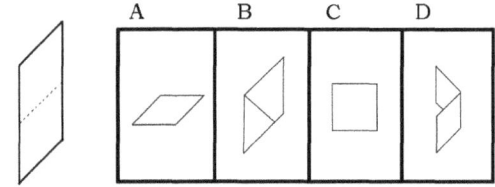

**34. When folded, what pattern is possible?**

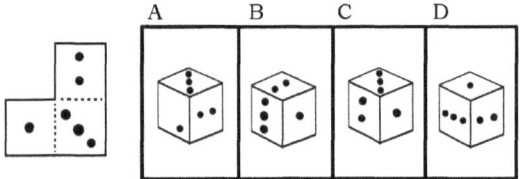

**35. When folded, what pattern is possible?**

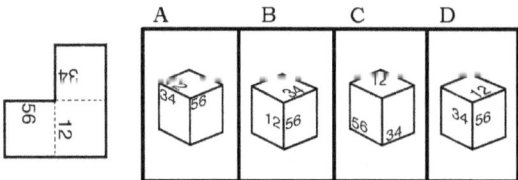

**36. When folded into a loop, what will the strip of paper look like?**

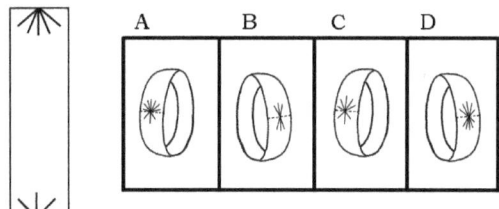

**37. Which of the choices is the same pattern at a different angle?**

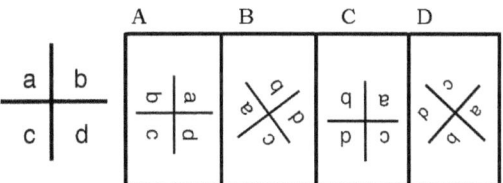

**38. When folded, what pattern is possible?**

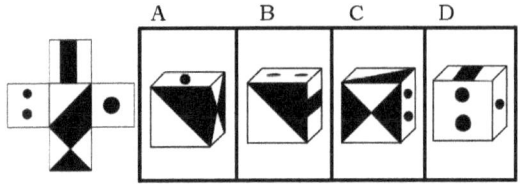

**39. When folded into a loop, what will the strip of paper look like?**

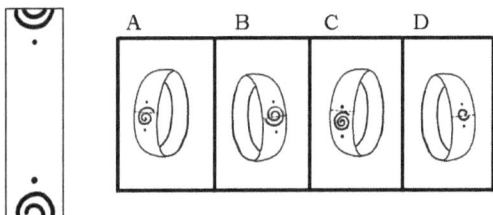

**40. When folded, what pattern is possible?**

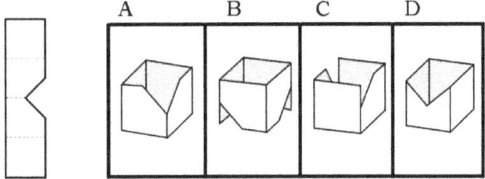

# Answer Key

## Reading - Part I - Vocabulary

**1. C**
Cut has the same meaning as gash.

**2. D**
Hazardous has the same meaning as dangerous.

**3. A**
Dark has the same meaning as shadowy.

**4. B**
Determine has the same meaning as choose.

**5. C**
Definite has the same meaning as clear.

**6. D**
Delectable has the same meaning as delicious.

**7. B**
Describe has the same meaning as portray.

**8. A**
Destroy has the same meaning as ruin.

**9. B**
Difference has the same meaning as dissimilarity.

**10. D**
Attain has the same meaning as achieve.

**11. A**
Boring has the same meaning as uninteresting.

**12. D**
Eager has the same meaning as enthusiastic.

**13. C**
End has the same meaning as stop.

**14. B**
Enjoy has the same meaning as delight in.

**15. C**
Elaborate has the same meaning as explain.

**16. A**
Truism: n. self evident or clear obvious truth.

**17. A**
Virago: Given to undue belligerence or ill manner at the slightest provocation; a shrew, a termagant.

**18. D**
Femur: n. The bone of the thigh or upper hind limb, articulating at the hip and the knee.

**19. C**
Genteel: Polite and well-mannered. Stylish or elegant. Aristocratic

20. A
Adulterate: v. To render (something) poorer in quality by adding another substance, typically an inferior one.

**Part II - Reading Comprehension**

**21. B**
The correct answer because that fact is stated directly in the passage. The passage explains that Anne taught Helen to hear by allowing her to feel the vibrations in her throat.

**22. A**
We can infer that Anne is a patient teacher because she did not leave or lose her temper when Helen bit or hit her; she just kept trying to teach Helen. Choice B is incorrect because Anne taught Helen to read and talk. Choice C is incorrect because Anne could hear. She was partially blind, not deaf. Choice D is incorrect because it does not have to do with patience.

**23. B**
The passage states that it was hard for anyone but Anne to

understand Helen when she spoke. Choice A is incorrect because the passage does not mention Helen spoke a foreign language. Choice C is incorrect because there is no mention of how quiet or loud Helen's voice was. Choice D is incorrect because we know from reading the passage that Helen did learn to speak.

**24. D**
This question tests the reader's summarization skills. The other choices A, B, and C focus on portions of the second paragraph that are too narrow and do not relate to the specific portion of text in question. The complexity of the sentence may mislead students into selecting one of these answers, but rearranging or restating the sentence will lead the reader to the correct answer. In addition, choice A makes an assumption that may or may not be true about the intentions of the company, choice B focuses on one product rather than the idea of the products, and choice C makes an assumption about women that may or may not be true and is not supported by the text.

**25. D**
This question tests the reader's summarization skills. The question is asking very generally about the message of the passage, and the title, "Ways Characters Communicate in Theater," is one indication of that. The other choices A, B, and C are all directly from the text, and therefore readers may be inclined to select one of them, but are too specific to encapsulate the entirety of the passage and its message.

**26. B**
The paragraph on soliloquies mentions "To be or not to be," and it is from the context of that paragraph that readers may understand that because "To be or not to be" is a soliloquy, Hamlet will be introspective, or thoughtful, while delivering it. It is true that actors deliver soliloquies alone, and may be "solitary" (choice A), but "thoughtful" (choice B) is more true to the overall idea of the paragraph. Readers may choose C because drama and theater can be used interchangeably and the passage mentions that soliloquies are unique to theater (and therefore drama), but this answer is not specific enough to the paragraph in question. Readers may pick up on the theme of life and death and Hamlet's true intentions

and select that he is "hopeless" (choice D), but those themes are not discussed either by this paragraph or passage, as a close textual reading and analysis confirms.

### 27. C
This question tests the reader's grammatical skills. Choice B seems logical, but parenthesis are actually considered to be a stronger break in a sentence than commas are, and along this line of thinking, actually disrupt the sentence more.

Choices A and D make comparisons between theater and film that are simply not made in the passage, and may or may not be true. This detail does clarify the statement that asides are most unique to theater by adding that it is not completely unique to theater, which may have been why the author didn't chose not to delete it and instead used parentheses to designate the detail's importance (choice C).

### 28. A
Low blood sugar occurs both in diabetics and healthy adults.

### 29. B
None of the statements are the author's opinion.

### 30. A
The author's purpose is the inform.

### 31. A
The only statement that is not a detail is, "A doctor can diagnosis this medical condition by asking the patient questions and testing."

### 32. A
This sentence is a recommendation.

### 33. C
Tips for a good night's sleep is the best alternative title for this article.

### 34. B
Mental activity is helpful for a good night's sleep is cannot be inferred from this article.

## 35. A
From the passage, one disadvantage of taking naps is they may keep you awake at night.

## 36. A
Based on the partial table of contents, this book is most likely about how to answer multiple choice.

## 37. C
To be infamous means to be remembered for an evil or terrible action. Therefore, the word infamy means to remember a bad or terrible thing. Choice A is incorrect because being famous is not the same as being infamous. Choice B is incorrect because the attack on Pearl Harbor was not good. Choice D is incorrect because Pearl Harbor was not forgotten.

## 38. C
Each answer choice except choice C contains the name of at least one country that was not part of the AXIS powers.

## 39. D
It is stated in the passage. Choice A is not correct because there was no indication that Japan would attack San Diego. Choice B is incorrect because the attack on Pearl Harbor was a surprise. Choice C is incorrect because Roosevelt was not planning to attack Japan.

## 40. C
The passage clearly states that Japan planned a surprise attack. They chose that early time to catch the U.S. military off guard. Choice A is incorrect because the military does not sleep late. Choice B is incorrect because there is no law against bombing countries. Choice D is incorrect because it makes no sense.

## 41. C
This question tests the reader's vocabulary skills. The uses of the negatives "but" and "less," especially right next to each other, may confuse readers into answering with choices A or D, which list words that are antonyms to "militant." Readers may also be confused by the comparison of healthy people with what is being described as an overly healthy person-

-both people are good, but the reader may look for which one is "worse" in the comparison, and therefore stray toward the antonym words. One key to understanding the meaning of "militant" if the reader is unfamiliar with it is to look at the root of the word; readers can then easily associate it with "military" and gain a sense of what the word signifies: defense (especially considered that the immune system defends the body). Choice C is correct over choice B because "militant" is an adjective, just as the words in choice C are, whereas the words in choice B are nouns.

**42. C**
This question tests the reader's understanding of function within writing. The other choices are details included surrounding the quoted text, and may therefore confuse the reader. A somewhat contradicts what is said earlier in the paragraph, which is that tests and treatments are improving, and probably doctors are along with them, but the paragraph doesn't actually mention doctors, and the subject of the question is the medicine. Choice B may seem correct to readers who aren't careful to understand that, while the author does mention the large number of people affected, the author is touching on the realities of living with allergies rather about the likelihood of curing all allergies. Similarly, while the author does mention the "balance" of the body, which is easily associated with "wholesome," the author is not really making an argument and especially is not making an extreme statement that allergy medicines should be outlawed. Again, because the article's tone is on living with allergies, choice C is an appropriate choice that fits with the title and content of the text.

**43. B**
This question tests the reader's inference skills. The text does not state who is doing the recommending, but the use of the "patients," as well as the general context of the passage, lends itself to the logical partner, "doctors," choice B. The author does mention the recommendation but doesn't present it as her own (i.e. "I recommend that"), so choice A may be eliminated. It may seem plausible that people with allergies (choice D) may recommend medicines or products to other people with allergies, but the text does not necessarily support this interaction taking place. Choice C may be

selected because the EpiPen is specifically mentioned, but the use of the phrase "such as" when it is introduced is not limiting enough to assume the recommendation is coming from its creators.

## 44. D
This question tests the reader's global understanding of the text. Choice D includes the main topics of the three body paragraphs, and isn't too focused on a specific aspect or quote from the text, as the other questions are, giving a skewed summary of what the author intended. The reader may be drawn to choice B because of the title of the passage and the use of words like "better," but the message of the passage is larger and more general than this.

## 45. B
Reading the document posted to the Human Resources website is optional.

## 46. B
The document is recommended changes and have not be implemented yet.

## 47. C
This question tests the reader's summarization skills. The use of the word "actually" in describing what kind of people poets are, as well as other moments like this, may lead readers to selecting choices B or D, but the author is more informing than trying to persuade readers. The author gives no indication that she loves poetry (choice B) or that people, students specifically (D), should write poems. Choice A is incorrect because the style and content of this paragraph do not match those of a foreword; forewords usually focus on the history or ideas of a specific poem to introduce it more fully and help it stand out against other poems. The author here focuses on several poems and gives broad statements. Instead, she tells a kind of story about poems, giving three very broad time periods in which to discuss them, thereby giving a brief history of poetry, as choice C states.

## 48. A
This question tests the reader's summarization skills. Key words in the topic sentences of each of the paragraphs ("old-

est," "Renaissance," "modern") should give the reader an idea that the author is moving chronologically. The opening and closing sentence-paragraphs are broad and talk generally. B seems reasonable, but epic poems are mentioned in two paragraphs, eliminating the idea that only new types of poems are used in each paragraph. Choice C is also easily eliminated because the author clearly mentions several different poets, groups of people, and poems. Choice D also seems reasonable, considering that the author does move from older forms of poetry to newer forms, but use of "so (that)" makes this statement false, for the author gives no indication that she is rushing (the paragraphs are about the same size) or that she prefers modern poetry.

**49. D**
This question tests the reader's attention to detail. The key word is "invented"--it ties together the Mesopotamians, who invented the written word, and the fact that they, as the inventors, also invented and used poetry. The other selections focus on other details mentioned in the passage, such as that the Renaissance's admiration of the Greeks (choice C) and that Beowulf is in Old English (choice A). Choice B may seem like an attractive answer because it is unlike the others and because the idea of heroes seems rooted in ancient and early civilizations.

**50. B**
This question tests the reader's vocabulary and contextualization skills. "Telling" is not an unusual word, but it may be used here in a way that is not familiar to readers, as an adjective rather than a verb in gerund form. A may seem like the obvious answer to a reader looking for a verb to match the use they are familiar with. If the reader understands that the word is being used as an adjective and that choice A is a ploy, they may opt to select choice D, "wordy," but it does not make sense in context. Choice C can be easily eliminated, and doesn't have any connection to the paragraph or passage. "Significant" (choice B) makes sense contextually, especially relative to the phrase "give insight" used later in the sentence.

## Section II - Language

## Part I - Spelling, Usage, Capitalization and Punctuation

**1. A**
The third conditional is used for talking about an unreal situation (a situation that did not happen) in the past. For example, "If I had studied harder, [if clause] I would have passed the exam" [main clause]. This has the same meaning as, "I failed the exam, because I didn't study hard enough."

**2. A**
Use a plural verb form for two subjects linked by "and."

**3. B**
In double negative sentences, one negative is replaced with "any."

**4. C**
"It's" is a contraction for it is or it has. "Its" is a possessive pronoun.

**5. A**
When two subjects are linked by "with" or "as well," use the verb form that matches the first subject.

**6. A**
The sentence requires the past perfect "has always been known." This is the only grammatically correct choice.

**7. C**
The superlative, "hottest," is used when expressing a temperature greater than that of anything to which it is being compared.

**8. D**
When comparing two items, use "the taller." When comparing more than two items, use "the tallest."

**9. B**
The past perfect form is used to describe an event that occurred in the past, and prior to another event. Here there are two things that happened, both of them in the past, and something the person wanted to do.

Event 1: Kiss came to town
Event 2: All the tickets sold out
What I wanted to do: Buy a ticket

The events are arranged:
When KISS came to town, all of the tickets **had been sold out** before I could buy one.

**10. A**
The subject is "rules" so the present tense plural form, "are," is used to agree with "realize."

**11. A**
"Who" is correct because the question uses an active construction. "To whom was first place given?" is a passive construction.

**12. D**
"Which" is correct, because the files are objects and not people.

**13. B**
Use a singular verb with either, each, neither, everyone and many.

**14. D**
Maintenance is the correct spelling.

**15. C**
Humorous is the correct spelling.

**16. A**
Mathematics is the correct spelling.

**17. A**
Use a comma to separate phrases.

## 18. A
The Sahara Desert is a proper name so capitalized. The names of countries, ie Africa are capitalized.

## 19. A
'She' is the simple subject of this sentence.

## 20. A
The simple predicate is 'studied long and hard.' The predicate of a sentence is the action performed by the subject.

## 21. B
This is an interrogative sentence.

## 22. C
It is not necessary to say the fish came from the topics, since we already know they are tropical.

## 23. B
The correct sentence is
Historians have been guessing for more than 100 years the doctor was a woman.

Here the phrase 'for more than 100 years' refers to how long historians have been guessing, and not to how long the doctor has been a woman.

## 24. B
Use a comma separates independent clauses. None of us wants to go to the party, not even if there will be live music.

## 25. A
This is an example where a comma appears before 'and,' but is disambiguating. Without the comma, the sentence would be "I own two dogs, a cat named Jeffrey and Henry, the goldfish." This means there is a cat named Jeffrey and Henry, and a goldfish with no name mentioned. The comma appears to show the distinction.
I own two dogs, a cat named Jeffrey, and Henry, the goldfish.

## 26. B
President is not capitalized unless used with a name as in,

President Obama.

**27. B**
'Jumped' is a verb. Verbs describe an action, state, or occurrence.

**28. B**
A confrontation is a head-on conflict, so a direct confrontation is redundant.

**29. D**
**Pesticide:** NOUN a substance, usually synthetic although sometimes biological, used to kill or contain the activities of pests.

**30. B**
**Hormones:** NOUN any substance produced by one tissue and conveyed by the bloodstream to another to effect physiological activity.

## Part II - Paragraphs

**1. D**
Suggested revision of sentence 1, "Humankind's thirst for knowledge is insatiable, making curiosity a driving force for advances throughout history."
Use the gender neutral "humankind. Replace the past perfect "has always been" with the present tense to make a simpler and more direct sentence. "Though history" is incorrect. Use "throughout" when referring to a time period. Replace the preposition "for" with "in."

**2. A**
Sentence 6 is the least relevant. "Curiosity was launched in late November 2011 from Cape Canaveral Air Force Station in Florida."

The third paragraph talks about the objectives of the rover. All sentences other than sentence 7 mention the objectives. This sentence, however, informs about when the spacecraft was launched.

## 3. A

Sentence 10 is least relevant to the main idea of the third paragraph. The following changes are suggested, "<u>To achieve its goals</u>, Curiosity has been engineered with cutting-edge technologies worth a budgetary expense exceeding 2.5 billion US dollars."

Clearly, the last paragraph talks about how Curiosity has been engineered to accomplish its objectives. The previous paragraph addressing the objectives of the rover, addition of the phrase "To achieve its goals," in choice A acts as a transition sentence between the paragraphs.

## 4. D

The changes needed to sentence 5 are, "So far, NASA has carried out several exploratory missions to Mars and the rover robot "Curiosity" is the latest and most sophisticated of all."

"Curiosity" is the name of a spacecraft that was assigned the particular name because of its association of its mission to satisfy our curiosity about the planet Mars. In this respect, the name bears a special meaning and emphasis, which must be reflected in representing it using the quotation mark.

Use of the adjective "exploratory" to describe the missions is correct.

Choice D offers these changes.

## 5. C

Sentence 11 is a fragment. "The discovery is significant because so far, no attempt has been made to use the abundant infrared radiation we receive throughout the year."

The fragment contains a subordinate clause derived from the complete thought "The discovery is significant because so far no attempt has been made to make use of the infra-red radiation that we receive in an abundant supply all throughout the year." It also contains the subject of the main clause, "The discovery," but does not have any verbal phrase for the main clause. Since the main clause remains incomplete, the thought is expressed in part. Therefore, it is a sentence fragment.

## 6. C
Sentence 9 can be deleted to reduce redundancy. "This is a major discovery in the solar power generation industry as it offers a cheap source of harnessing the Sun's energy."

Sentence 9 contributes to double redundancy; that is, it repeats two separate ideas. Along with repeating the cost-effective characteristic of the new discovery, it also reiterates the fact that it is a major discovery, both of which are unnecessary. It also interferes in the paragraph transition which can be established between sentence 8 and 10 if it is removed.

## 7. B
Suggested corrections to sentence 10, "Oleic acid, the main ingredient of olive oil, absorbs infra-red radiation, which is the major component of the Sun's radiation reaching the Earth."

The sentence is missing the subordinate conjunction "which" or "that" necessary to construct the subordinate clause, with a comma before "which." Choices B and C suggest these changes, but since choice C contains a punctuation error, only B is has the valid answer.

## 8. D
Suggested changes to sentence 2, "With continued concern over global climate change, environmentalists are urging governments to lower their dependence on fossil fuels to ensure reduced carbon emission into the atmosphere."

This sentence contains inappropriate use of gerunds and infinitives. To-infinitives are preferred when the continuous form of a main verb is used right before or after them. In this case, "urging" should be followed by the to-infinitive of "lower." Further across the sentence, the linking phrase "to," has only one acceptable form; itself. Therefore, the verb which is linked to must contain the infinitive form. The gerund form must be discarded. The only valid choice is D.

## 9. B
Suggested changes to sentence 6 are, "This information, coupled with conventional on-site procedures, help archeolo-

gists plan their excavation carefully and efficiently."
The second paragraph points out the significance of satellite imaging for archeological studies. The original sentence only makes a general claim. Choice A contradicts excavation principles by adding "along with a supply of heavy machinery" which would destroy the site. Choice B, more appropriately, adds the aspects of archeological excavation that are going to be boosted by the technology. Choices C and D offer very little relevance to satellite imaging and the dimensions of excavation that are going to be affected.

### 10. C
Sentence 9 can be re-written, "Different points in a civilization reflect IR radiation differently, provide detailed insight about the causes of these differing heat signatures."

This is a much shorter and more concise sentence which eliminates some details.

## Section III – Mathematics

### 1. B
First change all the terms to fractions, therefore, we get 7/3 / 7/5, to divide we need to invert the second fraction, 7/3 x 5/7, and then we cancel out to reduce to the lowest terms, 1/3 x 5/1 = 5/3, convert back to proper fraction to get 1 2/3

### 2. B
First, convert all the terms to fractions and then cancel out. Therefore, 2/3 x 11/7 x 21/4 = 2/3 x 11/1 x 3/4, 1/3 x 11/1 x 3/2, 1/1 x 11/1 x 1/2 = 11/2 = 5 1/2

### 3. A
First change all the terms to fractions, therefore, we get 21/5 / 7/3, to divide we need to invert the second fraction, 21/5 x 3/7, and then we cancel out to reduce to the lowest terms, 3/5 x 3/1 = 9/5, convert back to proper fraction to get 1 4/5

### 4. B
First, convert all the terms to fractions and then cancel out. Therefore, 10/3 x 9/4 x 16/5 = 10/1 x 3/4 x 16/5, 10/1 x 3/1 x 4/5, 2/1 x 3/1 x 4/1 = 24/1 = 24

**5. C**
First change all the terms to fractions, 28/9 / 8/3, to divide we need to invert the second fraction, 28/9 x 3/8, and then we cancel out to reduce to the lowest terms, 7/3 x 1/2 = 7/6, convert back to proper fraction to get 1 1/6

**6. B**
+(+) becomes a positive sign and -(-) equals +, therefore -9 + (+6) – (-2) = -9 + 6 + 2 = -3 + 2 = -1

**7. B**
There are 52 cards. Smith has 16 cards in which he can win. Therefore, his winning probability in a single game will be 16/52. Simon has 20 cards of wining so his probability of winning in single draw is 20/52. Simon will win more games.

**8. C**
This is an arithmetic series question where the 1st term is 18 and last term is 40. Expressing the question as a series, we have

18, 20, 22, 24, 26, 28, 30, 32, 34, 36, 38, 40
Therefore, after 11 days of practice he attains that 40 word per minute. As he practices 3 hours daily, the total number of hours required will be 33.

**9. C**
1 hour is equal to 3600 seconds and 1 kilometer is equal to 1000 meters. Therefore, a train covers 72000 meters in 36000 seconds.
Distance covered in 12 seconds = 12 × 72000/3600 = 240 meters.

**10. B**
Absent students = 83 – 72 = 11
Percent of absent students = 11/83 X 100 = 13.25
Reducing up to two significant digits will be 13.

| Day | Absent | Present | % Attendance |
|---|---|---|---|
| Monday | 5 | 40 | 88.88% |
| Tuesday | 9 | 36 | 80.00% |
| Wednesday | 4 | 41 | 91.11% |
| Thursday | 10 | 35 | 77.77% |
| Friday | 6 | 39 | 86.66% |

## 11. B
Time taken to travel from A to B in seconds = 3600 + (13 X 60) = 3600 + 780 = 4380 seconds.
Total time spent at traffic signals = 80 X 5 = 400 seconds.
The remaining driving time = 4380 − 400 = 3980 seconds = 3980/3600 = 1.106 hours
The speed will be 65/1.106 = 58.77 km/hr

## 12. C
Cash assets = 75600
Building assets after one year = 80500 X 1.1 = $88550
Machinery assets after one year = 125000 X 0.8 = 100,000
Total value of assets = 264150

## 13. C
Total earnings = 25000 + 500 + 860 = $26360
Food and Clothing expenses = 0.4 X 26360 = 10544
Children's education expense = 26360 X 0.1 = $2636
Utility Bills = $800
Savings = 26360 − 10544 − 2636 − 800 = $12380
Percent savings = 100 X 12380/26360 = 47%

## 14. B
1st prize winner receives, 7 X 1050/15 = $490
3rd price winner receives, 3 X 1050/15 = $210
Difference = 490 − 210 = $280

## 15. C
At 100% efficiency 1 machine produces 1450/10 = 145 m of cloth.

At 95% efficiency, 4 machines produce 4 * 145 * 95/100 = 551 m of cloth.

At 90% efficiency, 6 machines produce 6 * 145 * 90/100 = 783 m of cloth.

Total cloth produced by all 10 machines = 551 + 783 = 1334 m

Since the information provided and the question are based on 8 hours, we did not need to use time to reach the answer.

**16. D**
Distance covered by the car = 60 X 3.5 = 210 km.
Time required by the motorbike = 210/40 = 5.25 hr.

**17. C**
Let the grandson's age be X and the grandfather's age be Y.
According we have,
y = 8x
and
y + 6 = 5(x + 6)
Solving we get y = 64

**18. B**
5n + (19 – 2)) = 67, 5n + 17 = 67, 5n = 67 -17, 5n = 50, n = 50/5 = 10

**19. C**
The ratio between apples and oranges is 2 to 8 or 2:8. Bring to the lowest terms by dividing both sides by 2 gives 1:4.

**20. A**
The ratio between black and blue pens is 7 to 28 or 7:28. Bring to the lowest terms by dividing both sides by 7 gives 1:4.

**21. C**
X + 32 + 356 = 920. Therefore X + 388 = 920, X = 920 – 388 = 532

**22. B**
The ratio between green, red and blue candies is 3:12:9. Bring to the lowest terms by dividing the sides by 3 gives 1:4:3.

**23. A**
12 x 12 = 144, so 144/x =12, X = 12

**24. A**
34 x 2 = 68, so A – 68 = 18, A = 68 + 18 = 86

**25. D**
X% of 120 = 30, so X = 30/120 x 100/1 = 300/12 = 25

This questions can be estimated quickly just by looking at the numbers. 30 and 120 are related by, as 4 X 30 = 120. 4 expressed as a percent is 25%. Check quickly, 25% of 120 = 30.

**26. B**
X * 25% x 100 = 75, therefore, X * 25 = 75, X = 75/25 = 3

**27. D**
X% of 250 = 50, so X = 50/250 x 100/1= 100/5 = 20

**28. D**
Multiples of 3 are 3, 6, 9, 12 and Multiples of 4 are 4, 8, 12, Therefore the least common multiple is 12.

This can be estimated quickly. 3 is a prime number so the only possible multiples of 3 and any other number, say X, will be 3X.

**29. C**
The ratio between gold, silver and bronze coins is 2:6:8. Bring to the lowest terms by dividing each element in the original ratio by 2 gives 1:3:6.

**30. A**
Multiples of 8 are 8, 16, 24 and multiples of 12 are 12, 24, 36, so the least common multiple is 24.

**31. D**
3x = 20 + 7 = 27, x = 27/3, x = 9.

**32. C**
Multiples of 2 are 2, 4, 6 and Multiples of 3 are 3, 6, so the least common is 6.

**33. B**
124 = 12c - 20, 124 + 20 = 12c, 144 = 12c, c = 144/12 = 12.

**34. C**
Add the whole numbers and then add the fractions, therefore 3 + 5 {8/9 + 5/6}, then find a common denominator for the fractions 8 {16/18 + 15/18} = 8 31/18, then simplify to 9 13/18

**35. D**
Subtract the whole numbers and then subtract the fractions, therefore 7 - 2 {4/5 - 2/5}, the fractions has a common denominator, so
5 (4-2/5) = 5 2/5.

**36. A**
Three plus a number times 7 equals 42. Let X be the number.
(3 + X) times 7 = 42
7(3 + X) = 42

**37. C**
5205 / 25 = 208.20 or, approximately 208.

**38. D**
Two parallel lines(m & side AB) intersected by side AC
a = 50° (interior angles)

**39. A**
The wheel travels 2πr distance when it makes one revolution. Here, r stands for the radius. The radius is given as 25 cm in the figure. So,

2πr = 2π * 25 = 50π cm is the distance travelled in one revolution.

In 175 revolutions: 175 * 50π = 8750π cm is travelled.

We are asked to find the distance in meter.

1 m = 100 cm So;

8750π cm = 8750π / 100 = 87.5π m

**40. C**
Equilateral triangle with 9 cm sides
Perimeter = 9+9+9
= 27 cm.

**41. C**
In the figure, we are given a large circle and a small circle inside it; with the diameter equal to the radius of the large

one. The diameter of the small circle is 4 cm. This means that its radius is 2 cm. Since the diameter of the small circle is the radius of the large circle, the radius of the large circle is 4 cm. The area of a circle is calculated by: $\pi r^2$ where r is the radius.

Area of the small circle: $\pi(2)2 = 4\pi$

Area of the large circle: $\pi(4)2 = 16\pi$

The difference area is found by:

Area of the large circle - Area of the small circle = $16\pi - 4\pi = 12\pi$

## 42. C
Volume of a cylinder is $\pi \times r^2 \times h$
Diameter = 5 ft. so radius is 2.5 ft.
Volume of the cylinder = $\pi \times 2.5^2 \times 2$
= $\pi \times 6.25 \times 2 = 12.5 \pi$
Approximate $\pi$ to 3.142
Volume of the cylinder = 39.25

Volume of a rectangle = height X width X length.
= 5 X 5 X 4 = 100

Total volume = Volume of rectangular solid + volume of cylinder
Total volume = 100 + 39.25
Total volume = 139.25 ft$^3$ or approximately 140 ft$^3$

## 43. D
Two parallel lines intersected by a third line with angles of 75°
x = 75° (corresponding angles)
x + y = 180°(supplementary angles)
y = 180° - 75°
y = 105°

## 44. D
To find the total turnout in all three polling stations, we need to proportion the number of voters to the number of all registered voters.

Number of total voters = 945 + 860 + 1210 = 3015

Number of total registered voters = 1270 + 1050 + 1440 = 3760

Percentage turnout over all three polling stations = 3015 * 100/3760 = 80.19%

Checking the answers, we round 80.19 to the nearest whole number: 80%

**45. C**
Substitute the known terms, (3 x 2) + (4 x 4) x 8 =, 6 + 4 x 8=, 10 x 8 = 80

**46. B**
When multiplying exponent, add the exponents. Therefore $4^{2+7} = 4^9$

**47. A**
When dividing exponents, subtract the exponents. $10^{65-13} = 10^{52}$

**48. D**
Indonesia is growing the fastest at about 30%.

**49. D**
a. 0.4 portion of 200 = 80
b. 50% of 100 = 50
c. 0.06 portion of 2000 = 120
d. 2% of 1000 = 20
D is the smallest

**50. A**
5z = 52 – 10
Z = 10.4 – 2 (divide both sides by 5)
Z = 8.4

# Section IV -Ability

**1. D**
Each figure has one more square with a cross inside.

**2. C**
Two large square boxes and one small square box are inverted.

**3. B**
Every box has three black square boxes inside.

**4. D**
The shape with empty inside circle has been rotated counter-clockwise.

**5. A**
The colors of the two square boxes are reversed.

**6. B**
The sum of inside dots decreases by one.

**7. D**
The box is rotated and the shading reversed.

**8. B**
The number of sides increases by one.

**9. B**
The shape rotates clockwise.

**10. A**
The top and bottom rows cycle forward and the middle row cycles backward.

**11. D**
The sum of the top two numbers is divided by subtracting the bottom two numbers.

**12. C**
The black box goes to the bottom and the t symbol rotates.

**13. D**
The relation is the same figure rotated.

**14. D**
The shaded area is divided in half in the second figure.

**15. D**
The relation is the same figure rotated to the right.

**16. B**
The relation is the number of dots is one-half the number of sides.

**17. C**
The pattern is the same figure with a dot inside.

**18. A**
The relation is the same figure smaller, plus another figure with one more side.

**19. B**
The relation is the bottom half of the figure.

**20. C**
The relation is the right half of the first object.

**21. B**
The relation is the right half of the first object.

**22. B**
The first two figures have one-quarter of the area shaded. The figure given has one-half shaded which matches figure B.

**23. D**
Each figure has a smaller version if itself inside.

**24. A**
The figures are rotated 45 degrees.

**25. B**
**26. D**
**27. B**
**28. B**

29. A
30. A
31. C
32. B
33. D
34. C
35. D
36. C
37. D
38. A
39. B
40. A

# Practice Test Questions Set 2

THE QUESTIONS BELOW ARE NOT THE SAME AS YOU WILL FIND ON THE TACHS - THAT WOULD BE TOO EASY! And nobody knows what the questions will be and they change all the time. Below are general questions that cover the same subject areas as the TACHS. So, while the format and exact wording of the questions may differ slightly, and change from year to year, if you can answer the questions below, you will have no problem with the TACHS.

For the best results, take these practice test questions as if it were the real exam. Set aside time when you will not be disturbed, and a location that is quiet and free of distractions. Read the instructions carefully, read each question carefully, and answer to the best of your ability.

Use the bubble answer sheets provided. When you have completed the practice questions, check your answer against the Answer Key and read the explanation provided.

Do not attempt more than one set of practice test questions in one day. After completing the first practice test, wait two or three days before attempting the second set of questions.

**Section I – Reading**
**Questions:** 50
**Time:** 35 minutes

**Section II - Language**
**Questions:** 50
**Time:** 30 minutes

**Section III – Mathematics**
**Questions:** 50
**Time:** 40 Minutes

**Section IV - Ability**
**Questions:** 40
**Time:** 30 Minutes

# Reading Answer Sheet

|     | A | B | C | D | E |     | A | B | C | D | E |
|-----|---|---|---|---|---|-----|---|---|---|---|---|
| 1   | ○ | ○ | ○ | ○ | ○ | 26  | ○ | ○ | ○ | ○ | ○ |
| 2   | ○ | ○ | ○ | ○ | ○ | 27  | ○ | ○ | ○ | ○ | ○ |
| 3   | ○ | ○ | ○ | ○ | ○ | 28  | ○ | ○ | ○ | ○ | ○ |
| 4   | ○ | ○ | ○ | ○ | ○ | 29  | ○ | ○ | ○ | ○ | ○ |
| 5   | ○ | ○ | ○ | ○ | ○ | 30  | ○ | ○ | ○ | ○ | ○ |
| 6   | ○ | ○ | ○ | ○ | ○ | 31  | ○ | ○ | ○ | ○ | ○ |
| 7   | ○ | ○ | ○ | ○ | ○ | 32  | ○ | ○ | ○ | ○ | ○ |
| 8   | ○ | ○ | ○ | ○ | ○ | 33  | ○ | ○ | ○ | ○ | ○ |
| 9   | ○ | ○ | ○ | ○ | ○ | 34  | ○ | ○ | ○ | ○ | ○ |
| 10  | ○ | ○ | ○ | ○ | ○ | 35  | ○ | ○ | ○ | ○ | ○ |
| 11  | ○ | ○ | ○ | ○ | ○ | 36  | ○ | ○ | ○ | ○ | ○ |
| 12  | ○ | ○ | ○ | ○ | ○ | 37  | ○ | ○ | ○ | ○ | ○ |
| 13  | ○ | ○ | ○ | ○ | ○ | 38  | ○ | ○ | ○ | ○ | ○ |
| 14  | ○ | ○ | ○ | ○ | ○ | 39  | ○ | ○ | ○ | ○ | ○ |
| 15  | ○ | ○ | ○ | ○ | ○ | 40  | ○ | ○ | ○ | ○ | ○ |
| 16  | ○ | ○ | ○ | ○ | ○ | 41  | ○ | ○ | ○ | ○ | ○ |
| 17  | ○ | ○ | ○ | ○ | ○ | 42  | ○ | ○ | ○ | ○ | ○ |
| 18  | ○ | ○ | ○ | ○ | ○ | 43  | ○ | ○ | ○ | ○ | ○ |
| 19  | ○ | ○ | ○ | ○ | ○ | 44  | ○ | ○ | ○ | ○ | ○ |
| 20  | ○ | ○ | ○ | ○ | ○ | 45  | ○ | ○ | ○ | ○ | ○ |
| 21  | ○ | ○ | ○ | ○ | ○ | 46  | ○ | ○ | ○ | ○ | ○ |
| 22  | ○ | ○ | ○ | ○ | ○ | 47  | ○ | ○ | ○ | ○ | ○ |
| 23  | ○ | ○ | ○ | ○ | ○ | 48  | ○ | ○ | ○ | ○ | ○ |
| 24  | ○ | ○ | ○ | ○ | ○ | 49  | ○ | ○ | ○ | ○ | ○ |
| 25  | ○ | ○ | ○ | ○ | ○ | 50  | ○ | ○ | ○ | ○ | ○ |

# Language Answer Sheet

|   | A B C D E |    | A B C D E |
|---|-----------|----|-----------|
| 1 | ○○○○○ | 26 | ○○○○○ |
| 2 | ○○○○○ | 27 | ○○○○○ |
| 3 | ○○○○○ | 28 | ○○○○○ |
| 4 | ○○○○○ | 29 | ○○○○○ |
| 5 | ○○○○○ | 30 | ○○○○○ |
| 6 | ○○○○○ | 31 | ○○○○○ |
| 7 | ○○○○○ | 32 | ○○○○○ |
| 8 | ○○○○○ | 33 | ○○○○○ |
| 9 | ○○○○○ | 34 | ○○○○○ |
| 10 | ○○○○○ | 35 | ○○○○○ |
| 11 | ○○○○○ | 36 | ○○○○○ |
| 12 | ○○○○○ | 37 | ○○○○○ |
| 13 | ○○○○○ | 38 | ○○○○○ |
| 14 | ○○○○○ | 39 | ○○○○○ |
| 15 | ○○○○○ | 40 | ○○○○○ |
| 16 | ○○○○○ | 41 | ○○○○○ |
| 17 | ○○○○○ | 42 | ○○○○○ |
| 18 | ○○○○○ | 43 | ○○○○○ |
| 19 | ○○○○○ | 44 | ○○○○○ |
| 20 | ○○○○○ | 45 | ○○○○○ |
| 21 | ○○○○○ | 46 | ○○○○○ |
| 22 | ○○○○○ | 47 | ○○○○○ |
| 23 | ○○○○○ | 48 | ○○○○○ |
| 24 | ○○○○○ | 49 | ○○○○○ |
| 25 | ○○○○○ | 50 | ○○○○○ |

## Mathematics Answer Sheet

|    | A | B | C | D | E |     | A | B | C | D | E |
|----|---|---|---|---|---|-----|---|---|---|---|---|
| 1  | ○ | ○ | ○ | ○ | ○ | 26  | ○ | ○ | ○ | ○ | ○ |
| 2  | ○ | ○ | ○ | ○ | ○ | 27  | ○ | ○ | ○ | ○ | ○ |
| 3  | ○ | ○ | ○ | ○ | ○ | 28  | ○ | ○ | ○ | ○ | ○ |
| 4  | ○ | ○ | ○ | ○ | ○ | 29  | ○ | ○ | ○ | ○ | ○ |
| 5  | ○ | ○ | ○ | ○ | ○ | 30  | ○ | ○ | ○ | ○ | ○ |
| 6  | ○ | ○ | ○ | ○ | ○ | 31  | ○ | ○ | ○ | ○ | ○ |
| 7  | ○ | ○ | ○ | ○ | ○ | 32  | ○ | ○ | ○ | ○ | ○ |
| 8  | ○ | ○ | ○ | ○ | ○ | 33  | ○ | ○ | ○ | ○ | ○ |
| 9  | ○ | ○ | ○ | ○ | ○ | 34  | ○ | ○ | ○ | ○ | ○ |
| 10 | ○ | ○ | ○ | ○ | ○ | 35  | ○ | ○ | ○ | ○ | ○ |
| 11 | ○ | ○ | ○ | ○ | ○ | 36  | ○ | ○ | ○ | ○ | ○ |
| 12 | ○ | ○ | ○ | ○ | ○ | 37  | ○ | ○ | ○ | ○ | ○ |
| 13 | ○ | ○ | ○ | ○ | ○ | 38  | ○ | ○ | ○ | ○ | ○ |
| 14 | ○ | ○ | ○ | ○ | ○ | 39  | ○ | ○ | ○ | ○ | ○ |
| 15 | ○ | ○ | ○ | ○ | ○ | 40  | ○ | ○ | ○ | ○ | ○ |
| 16 | ○ | ○ | ○ | ○ | ○ | 41  | ○ | ○ | ○ | ○ | ○ |
| 17 | ○ | ○ | ○ | ○ | ○ | 42  | ○ | ○ | ○ | ○ | ○ |
| 18 | ○ | ○ | ○ | ○ | ○ | 43  | ○ | ○ | ○ | ○ | ○ |
| 19 | ○ | ○ | ○ | ○ | ○ | 44  | ○ | ○ | ○ | ○ | ○ |
| 20 | ○ | ○ | ○ | ○ | ○ | 45  | ○ | ○ | ○ | ○ | ○ |
| 21 | ○ | ○ | ○ | ○ | ○ | 46  | ○ | ○ | ○ | ○ | ○ |
| 22 | ○ | ○ | ○ | ○ | ○ | 47  | ○ | ○ | ○ | ○ | ○ |
| 23 | ○ | ○ | ○ | ○ | ○ | 48  | ○ | ○ | ○ | ○ | ○ |
| 24 | ○ | ○ | ○ | ○ | ○ | 49  | ○ | ○ | ○ | ○ | ○ |
| 25 | ○ | ○ | ○ | ○ | ○ | 50  | ○ | ○ | ○ | ○ | ○ |

# Ability Answer Sheet

|   | A | B | C | D | E |   |   | A | B | C | D | E |
|---|---|---|---|---|---|---|---|---|---|---|---|---|
| 1 | ○ | ○ | ○ | ○ | ○ |   | 26 | ○ | ○ | ○ | ○ | ○ |
| 2 | ○ | ○ | ○ | ○ | ○ |   | 27 | ○ | ○ | ○ | ○ | ○ |
| 3 | ○ | ○ | ○ | ○ | ○ |   | 28 | ○ | ○ | ○ | ○ | ○ |
| 4 | ○ | ○ | ○ | ○ | ○ |   | 29 | ○ | ○ | ○ | ○ | ○ |
| 5 | ○ | ○ | ○ | ○ | ○ |   | 30 | ○ | ○ | ○ | ○ | ○ |
| 6 | ○ | ○ | ○ | ○ | ○ |   | 31 | ○ | ○ | ○ | ○ | ○ |
| 7 | ○ | ○ | ○ | ○ | ○ |   | 32 | ○ | ○ | ○ | ○ | ○ |
| 8 | ○ | ○ | ○ | ○ | ○ |   | 33 | ○ | ○ | ○ | ○ | ○ |
| 9 | ○ | ○ | ○ | ○ | ○ |   | 34 | ○ | ○ | ○ | ○ | ○ |
| 10 | ○ | ○ | ○ | ○ | ○ |   | 35 | ○ | ○ | ○ | ○ | ○ |
| 11 | ○ | ○ | ○ | ○ | ○ |   | 36 | ○ | ○ | ○ | ○ | ○ |
| 12 | ○ | ○ | ○ | ○ | ○ |   | 37 | ○ | ○ | ○ | ○ | ○ |
| 13 | ○ | ○ | ○ | ○ | ○ |   | 38 | ○ | ○ | ○ | ○ | ○ |
| 14 | ○ | ○ | ○ | ○ | ○ |   | 39 | ○ | ○ | ○ | ○ | ○ |
| 15 | ○ | ○ | ○ | ○ | ○ |   | 40 | ○ | ○ | ○ | ○ | ○ |
| 16 | ○ | ○ | ○ | ○ | ○ |   | 41 | ○ | ○ | ○ | ○ | ○ |
| 17 | ○ | ○ | ○ | ○ | ○ |   | 42 | ○ | ○ | ○ | ○ | ○ |
| 18 | ○ | ○ | ○ | ○ | ○ |   | 43 | ○ | ○ | ○ | ○ | ○ |
| 19 | ○ | ○ | ○ | ○ | ○ |   | 44 | ○ | ○ | ○ | ○ | ○ |
| 20 | ○ | ○ | ○ | ○ | ○ |   | 45 | ○ | ○ | ○ | ○ | ○ |
| 21 | ○ | ○ | ○ | ○ | ○ |   | 46 | ○ | ○ | ○ | ○ | ○ |
| 22 | ○ | ○ | ○ | ○ | ○ |   | 47 | ○ | ○ | ○ | ○ | ○ |
| 23 | ○ | ○ | ○ | ○ | ○ |   | 48 | ○ | ○ | ○ | ○ | ○ |
| 24 | ○ | ○ | ○ | ○ | ○ |   | 49 | ○ | ○ | ○ | ○ | ○ |
| 25 | ○ | ○ | ○ | ○ | ○ |   | 50 | ○ | ○ | ○ | ○ | ○ |

## Section I – Reading

## Part I - Vocabulary

**Directions:** Choose the word that is closest in meaning to the underlined word.

**1. She has been to some very dangerous places. She is an <u>intrepid</u> explorer.**

   a. Brave

   b. Timid

   c. Timorous

   d. Cowardly


**2.  He wasn't especially generous. All the servings were very
<u>judicious</u>.**

   a. Abundant

   b. Careful

   c. Sparing

   d. Careless


**3. She presented a pretty good case up to now, but the latest evidence tends to <u>negate</u> everything he has said.**

   a. Disagree

   b. Reinforce

   c. Improve

   d. None of the above

**4. It is boring and I would rather not go, but the ceremony is obligatory.**

    a. Mandatory
    b. Optional
    c. Adaptable
    d. None of the above.

**5. We used that operating system 20 years ago, now it is obsolete.**

    a. Functional
    b. Disused
    c. Obese
    d. None of the Above.

**6. His bad manners really rankle me.**

    a. Annoy
    b. Obsucate
    c. Enliven
    d. None of the above.

**7. We don't want to hear the whole thing. Just the salient facts please.**

    a. Irrelevant
    b. Erroneous
    c. Relevant
    d. Trivial

**8. She works in a cubicle answering the phone all day. Her doctor says she is too <u>sedentary</u>.**

    a. Inactive
    b. Active
    c. Morbid
    d. None of the Above.

**9. We cannot reveal the source. It was posted by <u>anonymous</u>.**

    a. Unidentified
    b. Author
    c. Someone
    d. Nobody

**10. I have never seen anyone so rude. His behavior was <u>atrocious</u>.**

    a. Monstrous
    b. Perfect
    c. Unwarranted
    d. Suspicious

**11. I still don't know exactly. That isn't <u>conclusive</u> evidence.**

    a. Undeterred
    b. Unrelenting
    c. Unfortunate
    d. Definitive

**12. His investment scheme <u>duped</u> many serious investors, who lost money.**

    a. Helped
    b. Vindicated
    c. Fooled
    d. Reproved

**13. When we go to a party, we always <u>designate</u> a driver.**

    a. Feign
    b. Exploit
    c. Dote
    d. Appoint

**14. Choose the best definition of <u>specious</u>.**

    a. Logical
    b. Illogical
    c. Emotional
    d. 2 species

**15. Choose the best definition of proscribe.**

    a. Welcome
    b. Write a prescription
    c. Banish
    d. Give a diagnosis

**16. Fill in the blank.**

**When Craig's dog was struck by a car, he rushed his pet to the _____.**

   a. Emergency room
   b. Doctor
   c. Veterinarian
   d. Podiatrist

**17. Select another word for the underlined word in the sentence below.**

**She never made a mistake - her performance was always <u>impeccable</u>.**

   a. Charming
   b. Flattering
   c. Perfect
   d. Impervious

**18. Select the synonym of boisterous.**

   a. Loud
   b. Soft
   c. Gentle
   d. Warm

**19. Select the adjective that means hidden, secret, disguised.**

   a. Accustomed
   b. Covert
   c. Hide
   d. Carriage

**20. Select the verb that means straightforward, open and sincere.**

   a. Lawful
   b. Candid
   c. True
   d. Lawful

# Part III - Reading Comprehension

**Questions 21 - 24 refer to the following passage.**

**Passage 1 - The Crusades**

In 1095 Pope Urban II proclaimed the First Crusade with the intent and stated goal to restore Christian access to holy places in and around Jerusalem. Over the next 200 years there were 6 major crusades and numerous minor crusades in the fight for control of the "Holy Land." Historians are divided on the real purpose of the Crusades, some believing that it was part of a purely defensive war against Islamic conquest; some see them as part of a long-running conflict at the frontiers of Europe; and others see them as confident, aggressive, papal-led expansion attempts by Western Christendom. The impact of the crusades was profound, and judgment of the Crusaders ranges from laudatory to highly critical. However, all agree that the Crusades and wars waged during those crusades were brutal and often bloody. Several hundred thousand Roman Catholic Christians joined the Crusades, they were Christians from all over Europe.

Europe at the time was under the Feudal System, so while the Crusaders made vows to the Church they also were beholden to their Feudal Lords. This led to the Crusaders not only fighting the Saracen, the commonly used word for Muslim at the time, but also each other for power and economic gain in the Holy Land. This infighting between the Crusaders is why many historians hold the view that the Crusades were simply a front for Europe to invade the Holy Land for economic gain in the name of the Church. Another factor contributing to this theory is that while the army of crusaders marched towards Jerusalem they pillaged the land as they went. The church and feudal Lords vowing to return the land to its original beauty, and inhabitants, this rarely happened though as the Lords often kept the land for themselves. A full 800 years after the Crusades, Pope John Paul II expressed his sorrow for the massacre of innocent people and the lasting damage the Medieval church caused in that area of the World.

**21. What is the tone of this article?**

    a. Subjective

    b. Objective

    c. Persuasive

    d. None of the Above

**22. What can all historians agree on concerning the Crusades?**

    a. It achieved great things

    b. It stabilized the Holy Land

    c. It was bloody and brutal

    d. It helped defend Europe from the Byzantine Empire

**23. What impact did the feudal system have on the Crusades?**

    a. It unified the Crusaders

    b. It helped gather volunteers

    c. It had no effect on the Crusades

    d. It led to infighting, causing more damage than good

**24. What does Saracen mean?**

    a. Muslim

    b. Christian

    c. Knight

    d. Holy Land

**Questions 25 - 28 refer to the following passage.**

### ABC Electric Warranty

ABC Electric Company warrants that its products are free from defects in material and workmanship. Subject to the conditions and limitations set forth below, ABC Electric will, at its option, either repair or replace any part of its products that prove defective due to improper workmanship or materials.

This limited warranty does not cover any damage to the product from improper installation, accident, abuse, misuse, natural disaster, insufficient or excessive electrical supply, abnormal mechanical or environmental conditions, or any unauthorized disassembly, repair, or modification.

This limited warranty also does not apply to any product on which the original identification information has been altered, or removed, has not been handled or packaged correctly, or has been sold as second-hand.

This limited warranty covers only repair, replacement, refund or credit for defective ABC Electric products, as provided above.

**25. I tried to repair my ABC Electric blender, but could not, so can I get it repaired under this warranty?**

    a. Yes, the warranty still covers the blender

    b. No, the warranty does not cover the blender

    c. Uncertain. ABC Electric may or may not cover repairs under this warranty

**26. My ABC Electric fan is not working. Will ABC Electric provide a new one or repair this one?**

    a. ABC Electric will repair my fan

    b. ABC Electric will replace my fan

    c. ABC Electric could either replace or repair my fan can request either a replacement or a repair.

**27. My stove was damaged in a flood. Does this warranty cover my stove?**

    a. Yes, it is covered.

    b. No, it is not covered.

    c. It may or may not be covered.

    d. ABC Electric will decide if it is covered

**28. Which of the following is an example of improper workmanship?**

    a. Missing parts

    b. Defective parts

    c. Scratches on the front

    d. None of the above

**Questions 29 – 32 refer to the following passage.**

**Passage 2 - Women and Advertising**

Only in the last few generations have media messages been so widespread and so readily seen, heard, and read by so many people. Advertising is an important part of both selling and buying anything from soap to cereal to jeans. For whatever reason, more consumers are women than are men. Media message are subtle but powerful, and more attention has been paid lately to how these message affect women.
Of all the products that women buy, makeup, clothes, and other stylistic or cosmetic products are among the most popular. This means that companies focus their advertising on women, promising them that their product will make her

feel, look, or smell better than the next company's product will. This competition has resulted in advertising that is more and more ideal and less and less possible for everyday women. However, because women do look to these ideals and the products they represent as how they can potentially become, many women have developed unhealthy attitudes about themselves when they have failed to become those ideals.

In recent years, more companies have tried to change advertisements to be healthier for women. This includes featuring models of more sizes and addressing a huge outcry against unfair tools such as airbrushing and photo editing. There is debate about what the right balance between real and ideal is, because fashion is also considered art and some changes are made to purposefully elevate fashionable products and signify that they are creative, innovative, and the work of individual people. Artists want their freedom protected as much as women do, and advertising agencies are often caught in the middle.

Some claim that the companies who make these changes are not doing enough. Many people worry that there are still not enough models of different sizes and different ethnicities. Some people claim that companies use this healthier type of advertisement not for the good of women, but because they would like to sell products to the women who are looking for these kinds of messages. This is also a hard balance to find: companies do need to make money, and women do need to feel respected.
While the focus of this change has been on women, advertising can also affect men, and this change will hopefully be a lesson on media for all consumers.

**29. The second paragraph states that advertising focuses on women**

    a. to shape what the ideal should be

    b. because women buy makeup

    c. because women are easily persuaded

    d. because of the types of products that women buy

**30. According to the passage, fashion artists and female consumers are at odds because**

a. there is a debate going on and disagreement drives people apart

b. both of them are trying to protect their freedom to do something

c. artists want to elevate their products above the reach of women

d. women are creative, innovative, individual people

**31. The author uses the phrase "for whatever reason" in this passage to**

a. keep the focus of the paragraph on media messages and not on the differences between men and women

b. show that the reason for this is unimportant

c. argue that it is stupid that more women are consumers than men

d. show that he or she is tired of talking about why media messages are important

**32. This passage suggests that**

a. advertising companies are still working on making their messages better

b. all advertising companies seek to be more approachable for women

c. women are only buying from companies that respect them

d. artists could stop producing fashionable products if they feel bullied

**Questions 33 - 36 refer to the following passage.**

## FDR, the Treaty of Versailles, and the Fourteen Points

At the conclusion of World War I, those who had won the war and those who were forced to admit defeat welcomed the end of the war and expected that a peace treaty would be signed. The American president, Franklin D. Roosevelt, played an important part in proposing what the agreements should be and did so through his Fourteen Points.
World War I had begun in 1914 when an Austrian archduke was assassinated, leading to a domino effect that pulled the world's most powerful countries into war on a large scale. The war catalyzed the creation and use of deadly weapons that had not previously existed, resulting in a great loss of soldiers on both sides of the fighting. More than 9 million soldiers were killed.

The United States agreed to enter the war right before it ended, and many believed that its decision to become finally involved brought on the end of the war. FDR made it very clear that the U.S. was entering the war for moral reasons and had an agenda focused on world peace. The Fourteen Points were individual goals and ideas (focused on peace, free trade, open communication, and self reliance) that FDR wanted the power nations to strive for now that the war had concluded. He was optimistic and had many ideas about what could be accomplished through and during the post-war peace. However, FDR's fourteen points were poorly received when he presented them to the leaders of other world powers, many of whom wanted only to help their own countries and to punish the Germans for fueling the war, and they fell by the wayside. World War II was imminent, for Germany lost everything.

Some historians believe that the other leaders who participated in the Treaty of Versailles weren't receptive to the Fourteen Points because World War I was fought almost entirely on European soil, and the United States lost much less than did the other powers. FDR was in a unique position to determine the fate of the war, but doing it on his own terms did not help accomplish his goals. This is only one historical example of how the United State has tried to use its power as an important country, but found itself limited because of geological or ideological factors.

**33. The main idea of this passage is that**

    a. World War I was unfair because no fighting took place in America

    b. World War II happened because of the Treaty of Versailles

    c. the power the United States has to help other countries also prevents it from helping other countries

    d. Franklin D. Roosevelt was one of the United States' smartest presidents

**4. According to the second paragraph, World War I started because**

    a. an archduke was assassinated

    b. weapons that were more deadly had been developed

    c. a domino effect of allies agreeing to help each other

    d. the world's most powerful countries were large

**35. The author includes the detail that 9 million soldiers were killed**

    a. to demonstrate why European leaders were hesitant to accept peace

    b. to show the reader the dangers of deadly weapons

    c. to make the reader think about which countries lost the most soldiers

    d. to demonstrate why World War II was imminent

**36. According to this passage, it can be understood that the word catalyzed means**

a. analyzed
b. sped up
c. invented
d. funded

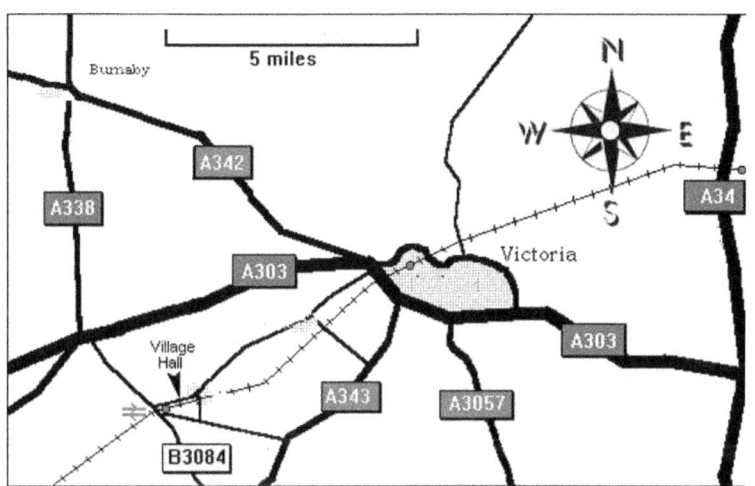

**37. Approximately how far is Victoria to Burnaby?**

a. About 10 miles
b. About 5 miles
c. About 15 miles
d. About 20 miles

**38. How is the Village Hall from Victoria?**

a. About 10 miles
b. About 5 miles
c. About 15 miles
d. About 20 miles

**Questions 39 - 42 refer to the following passage.**

**Chocolate Chip Cookies**

3/4 cup sugar
3/4 cup packed brown sugar
1 cup butter, softened
2 large eggs, beaten
1 teaspoon vanilla extract
2 1/4 cups all-purpose flour
1 teaspoon baking soda
3/4 teaspoon salt
2 cups semisweet chocolate chips
If desired, 1 cup chopped pecans, or chopped walnuts.
Preheat oven to 375 degrees.

Mix sugar, brown sugar, butter, vanilla and eggs in a large bowl. Stir in flour, baking soda, and salt. The dough will be very stiff.

Stir in chocolate chips by hand with a sturdy wooden spoon. Add the pecans, or other nuts, if desired. Stir until the chocolate chips and nuts are evenly dispersed.

Drop dough by rounded tablespoonfuls 2 inches apart onto a cookie sheet.

Bake 8 to 10 minutes or until light brown. Cookies may look underdone, but they will finish cooking after you take them out of the oven.

**39. What is the correct order for adding these ingredients?**

    a. Brown sugar, baking soda, chocolate chips
    b. Baking soda, brown sugar, chocolate chips
    c. Chocolate chips, baking soda, brown sugar
    d. Baking soda, chocolate chips, brown sugar

### 40. What does sturdy mean?

   a. Long
   b. Strong
   c. Short
   d. Wide

### 41. What does disperse mean?

   a. Scatter
   b. To form a ball
   c. To stir
   d. To beat

### 42. When can you stop stirring the nuts?

   a. When the cookies are cooked.
   b. When the nuts are evenly distributed.
   c. When the nuts are added.
   d. After the chocolate chips are added.

**Questions 43 - 46 refer to the following passage.**

**Passage 5 - Frankenstein**

Great God! What a scene has just taken place! I am yet dizzy with the remembrance of it. I hardly know whether I shall have the power to detail it; yet the tale which I have recorded would be incomplete without this final and wonderful catastrophe. I entered the cabin where lay the remains of my ill-fated and admirable friend. Over him hung a form which I cannot find words to describe—gigantic in stature, yet uncouth and distorted in its proportions. As he hung over the coffin, his face was concealed by long locks of ragged hair; but one vast hand was extended, in color and apparent texture like that of a mummy. When he heard the sound of my approach, he ceased to utter exclamations of grief and horror and sprung towards the window. Never did I behold a vision so horrible as his face, of such loathsome yet appalling hideousness. I shut my eyes involuntarily and endeavored to recollect what were my duties with regard to this destroyer. I called on him to stay.

He paused, looking on me with wonder, and again turning towards the lifeless form of his creator, he seemed to forget my presence, and every feature and gesture seemed instigated by the wildest rage of some uncontrollable passion.

"That is also my victim!" he exclaimed. "In his murder my crimes are consummated; the miserable series of my being is wound to its close! Oh, Frankenstein! Generous and self-devoted being! What does it avail that I now ask thee to pardon me? I, who irretrievably destroyed thee by destroying all thou lovedst. Alas! He is cold, he cannot answer me."

His voice seemed suffocated, and my first impulses, which had suggested to me the duty of obeying the dying request of my friend in destroying his enemy, were now suspended by a mixture of curiosity and compassion. I approached this tremendous being; I dared not again raise my eyes to his face, there was something so scaring and unearthly in his ugliness. I attempted to speak, but the words died away on my lips. The monster continued to utter wild and incoherent self-reproaches. At length I gathered resolution to address him in a pause of the tempest of his passion.

"Your repentance," I said, "is now superfluous. If you had listened to the voice of conscience and heeded the stings of remorse before you had urged your diabolical vengeance to this extremity, Frankenstein would yet have lived."

**43. Who is the "ill-fated and admirable friend" who is lying in the coffin?**

    a. Frankenstein's monster

    b. Frankenstein

    c. Mary Shelley

    d. Unknown

**44. Why is the speaker 'suspended" from following through on his duty to destroy the monster?**

   a. The way the monster looks

   b. The monster's remorse

   c. Curiosity and compassion

   d. Fear the monster might kill him too

**45. How does Frankenstein's monster destroy Frankenstein?**

   a. By killing Frankenstein

   b. By letting himself be the monster everyone sees him as

   c. By destroying everything Frankenstein loved

   d. All of the above

**46. When the Speaker says the monster's repentance is "superfluous, what does he mean?**

   a. That it is unnecessary and unused because Frankenstein is already dead and cannot hear him

   b. That he accepts the repentance on behalf of Frankenstein

   c. That the monster does not actually feel remorseful

   d. That his repentance is unneeded because he did not do anything wrong

**Questions 47 - 50 refer to the following passage.**

**Lowest Price Guarantee**

**Get it for less. Guaranteed!**

ABC Electric will beat any advertised price by 10% of the difference.

   1) If you find a lower advertised price, we will beat it by 10% of the difference.

2) If you find a lower advertised price within 30 days* of your purchase we will beat it by 10% of the difference.

3) If our own price is reduced within 30 days* of your purchase, bring in your receipt and we will refund the difference.

*14 days for computers, monitors, printers, laptops, tablets, cellular & wireless devices, home security products, projectors, camcorders, digital cameras, radar detectors, portable DVD players, DJ and pro-audio equipment, and air conditioners.

**47. I bought a radar detector 15 days ago and saw an ad for the same model only cheaper. Can I get 10% of the difference refunded?**

    a. Yes. Since it is less than 30 days, you can get 10% of the difference refunded.

    b. No. Since it is more than 14 days, you cannot get 10% of the difference re-funded.

    c. It depends on the cashier.

    d. Yes. You can get the difference refunded.

**48. I bought a flat-screen TV for $500 10 days ago and found an advertisement for the same TV, at another store, on sale for $400. How much will ABC refund under this guarantee?**

    a. $100
    b. $110
    c. $10
    d. $400

**49. What is the purpose of this passage?**

    a. To inform
    b. To educate
    c. To persuade
    d. To entertain

**Questions 50 refers to the following passage.**

### Passage 6 - What Is Mardi Gras?

Mardi Gras is fast becoming one of the South's most famous and most celebrated holidays. The word Mardi Gras comes from the French and the literal translation is "Fat Tuesday." The holiday has also been called Shrove Tuesday, due to its associations with Lent. The purpose of Mardi Gras is to celebrate and enjoy before the Lenten season of fasting and repentance begins.

What originated by the French Explorers in New Orleans, Louisiana in the 17th century is now celebrated all over the world. Panama, Italy, Belgium and Brazil all host large scale Mardi Gras celebrations, and many smaller cities and towns celebrate this fun loving Tuesday as well. Usually held in February or early March, Mardi Gras is a day of extravagance, a day for people to eat, drink and be merry, to wear costumes, masks and to dance to jazz music.
The French explorers on the Mississippi River would be in shock today if they saw the opulence of the parades and floats that grace the New Orleans streets during Mardi Gras these days. Parades in New Orleans are divided by organizations. These are more commonly known as Krewes.

Being a member of a Krewe is quite a task because Krewes are responsible for overseeing the parades. Each Krewe's parade is ruled by a Mardi Gras "King and Queen." The role of the King and Queen is to "bestow" gifts on their adoring fans as the floats ride along the street. They throw doubloons, which is fake money and usually colored green, purple and gold, which are the colors of Mardi Gras. Beads in those color shades are also thrown and cups are thrown as well. Beads are by far the most popular souvenir of any Mardi Gras parade, with each spectator attempting to gather as many as possible.

**50. The purpose of Mardi Gras is to**

    a. Repent for a month.

    b. Celebrate in extravagant ways.

    c. Be a member of a Krewe.

    d. Explore the Mississippi.

## Section II - Language

## Part I - Spelling, Capitalization, Punctuation, and Usage

**1. Elaine promised to bring the camera _____ at the mall yesterday.**

    a. by me

    b. with me

    c. at me

    d. to me

**2. Last night, he _____ the sleeping bag down beside my mattress.**

    a. lay

    b. laid

    c. lain

    d. has laid

**3. I would have bought the shirt for you if**

    a. I had known you liked it.

    b. I have known you liked it.

    c. I would know you liked it.

    d. I know you liked it.

**4. Many believers still hope _____ proof of the existence of ghosts.**

    a. two find
    b. to find
    c. to found
    d. to have been found

**5. Choose the sentence with the correct grammar.**

    a. The court summons was placed on his desk
    b. The court summons are placed on his desk
    c. The court summons were placed on his desk
    d. None of the above

**6. To _____, Anne was on time for her math class.**

    a. everybody's surprise
    b. every body's surprise
    c. everybodys surprise
    d. everybodys' surprise

**7. As an added bonus, we got to see the orchestra warm up.**

**What part of this sentence is redundant?**

    a. Added
    b. Bonus
    c. Warm up
    d. None of the above

**8. If he _____ the textbook like he was supposed to, he would have known what was on the test.**

    a. will have read
    b. shouldn't have read
    c. would have read
    d. had read

**9. Following the tornado, telephone poles _____ all over the street.**

    a. laid
    b. lied
    c. were lying
    d. were laying

**10. In Edgar Allen Poe's _____ Edgar Allen Poe describes a man with a guilty conscience.**

    a. short story, "The Tell-Tale Heart,"
    b. short story The Tell-Tale Heart,
    c. short story, The Tell-Tale Heart
    d. short story. "the Tell-Tale Heart,"

**11. Billboards are considered an important part of advertising for big business, _____ by their critics.**

    a. but, an eyesore;
    b. but, " an eyesore,"
    c. but an eyesore
    d. but-an eyesore-

**12. I can never remember how to use those two common words, "sell," meaning to trade a product for money, or _____ meaning an event where products are traded for less money than usual.**

    a. sale-
    b. "sale,"
    c. "sale
    d. "to sale,"

**13. Choose the sentence with the correct grammar.**

    a. Neither the teacher nor the students is left in class.
    b. Neither the teacher nor the students was left in class.
    c. Neither the teacher nor the students are left in class.
    d. None of the above.

**14. The class just finished reading _____ a short story by Carl Stephenson about a plantation owner's battle with army ants.**

    a. -"Leinengen versus the Ants,"
    b. Leinengen versus the Ants,
    c. "Leinengen versus the Ants,"
    d. Leinengen versus the Ants

**15. After the car was fixed, it _____ again.**

    a. ran good
    b. ran well
    c. would have run well
    d. ran more well

**16. "Where does the sun go during the _____ asked little Kathy.**

    a. night,"
    b. night"?,
    c. night,?"
    d. night?"

**17. Choose the correct spelling.**

    a. conscentious
    b. conscientios
    c. conscientious
    d. consceintious

**18. I have finished studying for today.**

**What type of sentence is this?**

    a. Imperative
    b. Interrogative
    c. Exclamatory
    d. Declarative

**19. Which of the following sentences contains a redundant phrase?**

    a. I haven't seen her for ages.
    b. My suitcase is books all the way to Amsterdam.
    c. The end result was very disappointing.
    d. None of the above.

## 20. Choose the correct sentence.

a. Their only employee with a nose ring is a young man named Daniel.

b. Their only employee is a young man named Daniel with a nose ring.

c. Their only employee is a young man with a nose ring named Daniel.

d. A and C are correct.

## 21. Choose the sentence with the correct grammar.

a. Everyone are to wear a black tie.

b. Everyone have to wear a black tie.

c. Everyone has to wear a black tie.

d. None of the above.

## 22. Choose the correct spelling.

a. leisuire

b. lesure

c. lesure

d. leisure

## 23. Choose the correct spelling.

a. pigeone

b. pigoen

c. pigeon

d. pidgeon

## 24. Choose the correct spelling.

a. odyessy

b. odeyssey

c. odysey

d. odyssey

**25. Choose the sentence with the correct grammar.**

    a. The salmon has been cooked.
    b. The salmon have been cooked.
    c. Both of the above.
    d. None of the above.

**26. This is absolutely incredible \_\_\_\_**

    a. !
    b. .
    c. :
    d. ;

**27. Watch out for the broken glass \_\_\_\_**

    a. .
    b. ?
    c. ,
    d. !

**28. I still don't know exactly. That isn't _____ evidence.**

    a. Undeterred
    b. Unrelenting
    c. Unfortunate
    d. Conclusive

**29. He walked all the way downtown.**

**What is the simple subject of this sentence?**

    **a.** He
    b. Walked
    c. Downtown
    d. All the way

**30.** He could manipulate the coins in his fingers very

    a. Brazenly

    b. Eloquently

    c. Boisterously

    d. Deftly

# Part II - Paragraphs

# Leg Surgery

The main reason many young women opt for surgery, despite the pain, inconvenience and cost, is the height discrimination in an increasingly competitive job market. [1] Almost all firms put certain height criteria for the candidates who apply. [2] For example, for an air stewardess position, women must be no more than 163 cm tall; whereas for jobs in foreign affairs, Chinese diplomats are required to match their foreign counterparts. [3] Height concerns also effect routine citizenship privileges such as driving licenses, which require a height of at least 157 cm to be eligible for taking the test in some places. [4]

The urge to undergo surgery is becoming increasingly popular among Chinese males as well. [5] "It offers me a 10 cm increase in my height, which can dramatically change my future," says Jing Yong, an interpreter working in Hong Kong. [6] "This will allow me better opportunities in the competitive job market here," adds the young multilingual who couldn't make it to the foreign ministry for being below 168 cm. [7]
Even parents approve of the idea, being fully aware of all the complexity and they are willing to finance such a labyrinth surgery. [8] "It's something that will give her confidence and achieve her goals in life. [9] Her height used to bother her tremendously, now this can change that," comments Swee Jing's father by her bedside as she is recovering from the eighteen-months process that involves elongating her tibia and fibula by placing two rods that will stimulate the extra growth of the bones. [10] They too are hopeful about the possibilities the surgery would affect the life of their daughter. [11]

**31. Which sentence in the second paragraph is least relevant to the main idea of the first paragraph?**

    a. 2
    b. 3
    c. 4
    d. 5

**32. Which sentence is not consistent with the author's purpose?**

    a. 3
    b. 6
    c. 9
    d. 12

**33. Which of the following sentences, if inserted after sentence 7, would best illustrate the main idea of the passage?**

    a. This is the main reason I am willing to undergo this surgery

    b. This artificial way of gaining height is turning out to be a new trend among the new generation in height conscious China.

    c. Height is a very big problem for Chinese people, particularly for those who wish to go abroad and carry the flag of China there.

    d. Young people like Yong will have to spend the rest of their lives with a fake pair of legs though.

**34. Which of the following changes are needed in sentence 8?**

   a. Even parents approve of the idea, being fully aware of all the sophistications and they are willing to finance such a labyrinth surgery.

   b. Even parents approve of the idea, being fully aware of all the complications and they are willing to finance such a sophisticated surgery.

   c. Even parents approve of the idea, being fully aware of all the complexity and they are willing to finance such a sophisticated surgery.

   d. Even parents approve of the idea, being fully aware of all the complexity and they are willing to finance such a sophisticated surgery.

# My Friend Luke

My forty-year old friend Luke is possibly the sweetest, shyest person enjoying his life on the entire Earth. [1] He is somewhat short, skinny and upright; has a thin moustache and a thinner trace of hair covering his head. [2] And since he has problems seeing distant things, he wears glasses that are small, thick and frameless; the round coffee-brown colored glasses give him a cool appearance uniquely suited to his personality. [3] Which I doubt belongs to any other person. [4]

There are traits in him seldom found in others. [5] While in a crowd, he walks sideways so as not to trouble others. [6] Instead of requesting a space to move ahead, he glides past to one side of the person blocking in his way. [7] If the gap turns out to be so narrow that it does not permit his bony frame to pass, he waits patiently for the person to move out of the way. [8] He is panicked by street dogs and neighbors' cats and in order to avoid them, he crosses to the other side of the street every now and then. [9]

Luke never speaks, as he thinks speaking is a waste of energy; something he is vehemently dedicated to saving. [10] Whenever he does, in order not to interrupt anybody, he speaks with a very soft, low tone – in a way no one ever notices him speaking in the first place. [11] Quite ironically, when he gets a rare chance to speak, he never succeeds in speaking more than two words before being interrupted by others. [12]

**35. What sentence from the passage is an example of a sentence fragment?**

    a. 4
    b. 5
    c. 6
    d. 7

**36. Which sentence in the second paragraph is least relevant to the main idea of the second paragraph?**

    a. 6
    b. 7
    c. 8
    d. 9

**37. Which of the following sentences should be modified to reduce redundancy?**

    a. 2
    b. 3
    c. 4
    d. 5

## Spiderman

Spiders have always fascinated Johnson. [1] Ever since his childhood visit to his grandfather's farm in Vancouver where he first saw them in a large web that almost covered the gate of the granary warehouse, he looked for spiders everywhere he visited. [2] He would search for spider webs even in the high rise apartments such as the one he lives in now. [3] He would find them there too. [4] Hanging between two walls near one corner of the store room, a magnificent piece of art left half woven and still being worked on. [5]

It is not the life of the spiders itself that attracted Johnson, rather their art. [6] He likes their delicate webs. [7] The amazing shape and sizes of the webs. [8] The symmetry, the balance, the intricate design and the detailed network fascinates him. [9] He wanders how they manage to create something unique like this with such a little brain that they have. [10] That is why he likes to catch them in action, while they are weaving. [11]

When he opened the store room this week, he saw the huge web in the left corner touching the roof. [12] That has been there for almost six months now and it lay there as it were last month. [13] No strands added. [14] It took on a grayish shade from the dust it gathered over the weeks, making it obvious that Binny has stopped working on it. [15] Hanging here and there in the web are some dry mosquitoes that were spared by the monster that owns the trap. [16]

In the far left, on the wall adjacent to the door, Johnson is trying to build a web out of string and glue -without much success! [17] "Incredible, you little genius!" Johnson murmurs to himself. [18]

In the far left, on the wall adjacent to the door, Johnson is trying to build a web out of string and glue -without much success! [17] "Incredible, you little genius!" Johnson murmurs to himself. [18]

**38. What sentence from the passage is an example of a sentence fragment?**

    a. 2
    b. 3
    c. 4
    d. 5

**39. Which of the following changes would focus attention on the main idea of the second paragraph?**

    a. He finds the webs to be magnificent piece of art.

    b. He is more interested in the web that they weave.

    c. He enjoys the webs that they weave.

    d. He wanders about the webs that they weave.

**40. Which of the following are needed in the sentence 10?**

    a. He wonders how they manage to create something so unique with such a tiny brain.

    b. He ponders how they manage to create something unique like this with such a tiny brain.

    c. He imagines how they manage to create something unique like this with such a tiny brain.

    d. He questions how they manage to create something unique like this with such a little brain that they have.

## Section IV – Math

**1. The sum of the digits of a 2-digit number is 12. If we switch the digits, the number we get will be greater than the initial one by 36. Find the initial number.**

    a. 39
    b. 48
    c. 57
    d. 75

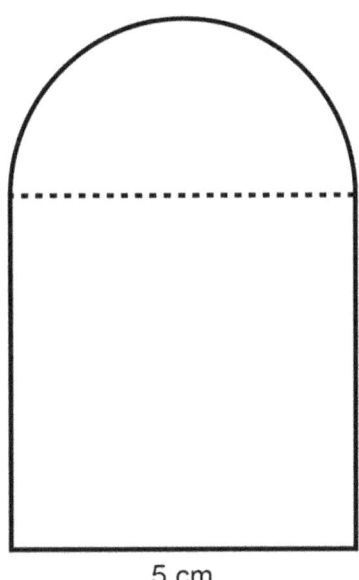

5 cm

**Note:** figure not drawn to scale

**2. What is the perimeter of the above shape, assuming the bottom portion is square?**

    a. 17.5 π cm
    b. 20 π cm
    c. 15 π cm
    d. 25 π cm

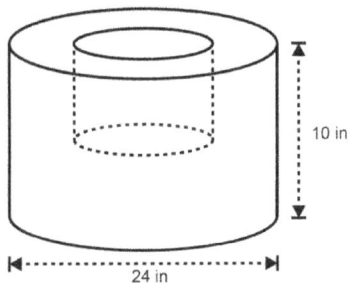

**Note:** figure not drawn to scale

3. What is the volume of the above solid made by a hollow cylinder that is half the size (in all dimensions) of the larger cylinder?

    a. 1440 π in³
    b. 1260 π in³
    c. 1040 π in³
    d. 960 π in³

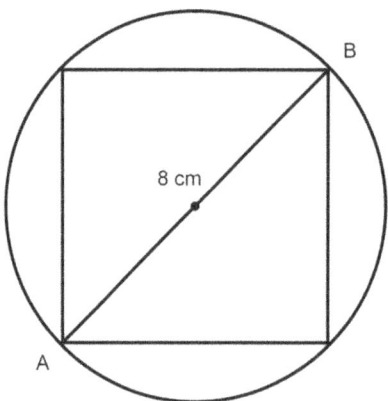

**Note:** figure not drawn to scale

4. What is area of the circle?

    a. 4 π cm²
    b. 12 π cm²
    c. 10 π cm²
    d. 16 π cm²

5. John jogs around a 75-meter diameter track 7 times. How much linear distance did he cover?

   a. 1250 meters
   b. 1450 meters
   c. 1650 meters
   d. 1725 meters

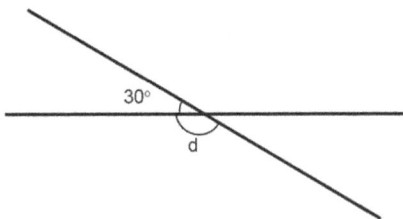

6. What is the indicated angle above?

   a. 150°
   b. 330°
   c. 60°
   d. 120°

7. On a circular jogging track with a circumference of 1.2 km, John, Tony and David walk at the rate of 120, 100 and 75 meters per minute respectively. If they all start walking in the same direction, how long will it take until they are together again?

   a. 200 minutes
   b. 220 minutes
   c. 240 minutes
   d. 260 minutes

**8. On a scaled map, city A is 12.4 cm away from city B. If the scale is 1 cm = 5 km then what is the actual distance between these two cities?**

    a. 12.4 km
    b. 48.4 km
    c. 58 km
    d. 62 km

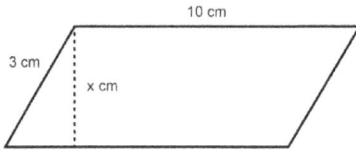

**Note:** figure not drawn to scale

**9. What is the perimeter of the parallelogram above?**

    a. 12 cm
    b. 26 cm
    c. 13 cm
    d. (13+x) cm

**10. Estimate 2009 x 108.**

    a. 110,000
    b. 2,0000
    c. 21,000
    d. 210,000

11. The playing times for three songs on a compact disc are as follows: 4 minutes 56 seconds for song A, 2 minutes 30 seconds for song B, 10 minutes 16 seconds for song C. What is the average playing time for the three songs?

    a. 17 minutes 42 seconds
    b. 6 minutes 7 seconds
    c. 6 minutes
    d. 5 minutes 54 seconds

12. John is a barber and receives 40% of the amount paid by his customers, and all the tips. If a customer pays $8.50 for a haircut and leaves a tip of $1.30, how much money does John receive?

    a. $3.92
    b. $4.70
    c. $5.30
    d. $6.40

13. The length of a rectangle is 5 in. more than its width. The perimeter of the rectangle is 26 in. What is the width and length of the rectangle?

    a. Width 6 in., Length 9 in.
    b. Width 4 in., Length 9 in.
    c. Width 4 in., Length 5 in.
    d. Width 6 in., Length 11 in.

14. Calculate $(3a + 4b) * d$ when A = 2, b = 4 and d = 8

    a. 40
    b. 150
    c. 112
    d. 176

15. c = 4, n = 5 and x = 3. Calculate 2cnx/2n

   a. 12
   b. 50
   c. 8
   d. 21

16. Simplify 3 1/2 / 2 4/5

   a. 1 1/4
   b. 2 1/4
   c. 1 1/3
   d. 2 1/3

17. Solve 2b/3 + 3a/5 − 2, where b = 9 and a = 10

   a. 5
   b. 10
   c. 20
   d. 9

18. Simplify (1/3 + 2/6) - (3/4 - 1/3)

   a. 1/4
   b. 5/11
   c. 3/7
   d. 2/9

19. Simplify (4/5 - 3/10) + (2/3 − 3/9) =

   a. 4/11
   b. 5/6
   c. 7/15
   d. 9/11

**20. Translate the following into an equation: 2 + a number divided by 7.**

    a. (2 + X)/7
    b. (7 + X)/2
    c. (2 + 7)/X
    d. 2/(7 + X)

**21. If a = 12 and b = 8, solve 6b - a + 2a**

    a. 12/9
    b. 18
    c. 16
    d. 12

**22. Simplify 3 2/3 - 1 2/8**

    a. 3/5
    b. 3/5
    c. 2 5/12
    d. 1 5/12

**23. Simplify 7 2/5 – 4 3/10**

    a. 3 1/10
    b. 3 2/5
    c. 4 1/5
    d. 3 7/10

**24. Solve for x. -5 – 5x = 8x + 8**

    a. 6
    b. 3
    c. 1
    d. 2

**25. Solve 2 1/3 x 1 3/7 x 3/4**

   a. 2 1/2
   b. 9
   c. 3 2/3
   d. 2 2/5

**26. Simplify 7 4/5 − 4 2/3**

   a. 4 2/5
   b. 3 2/15
   c. 3 7/15
   d. 4 3/5

**27. Solve for x.  12x - 8 = 3x + 10**

   a. 6
   b. 4
   c. 2
   d. 3

**28. Simplify (3/5 - 2/5) + (3/4 − 2/8)**

   a. 18/45
   b. 7/11
   c. 14/20
   d. 12/19

**29. Solve for a.  6a + 4 = 28 + 2a**

   a. 4
   b. 8
   c. 2
   d. 6

**30. Simplify (3/4 - 1/4) - (3/5 – 2/5)**

  a. 9/20
  b. 4/15
  c. 7/15
  d. 11/20

**31. Solve for x. 6 + 9x = 12 + 7x**

  a. 5
  b. 2
  c. 4
  d. 3

**32. Simplify 6 2/5 / 2 2/7**

  a. 2 1/4
  b. 1 1/5
  c. 2 4/5
  d. 2 2/3

**33. Solve for a. -6 + 7a = 9 + 4a**

  a. 3
  b. 5
  c. 2
  d. 6

**34. A square lawn has an area of 62,500 square meters. What is the cost of building fence around it at a rate of $5.5 per meter?**

  a. $4000
  b. $4500
  c. $5000
  d. $5500

**35.** The following numbers are the ages of people on a bus – 3, 6, 27, 13, 6, 8, 12, 20, 5, 10. Calculate their average of their ages.

    a. 11
    b. 6
    c. 9
    d. 110

**36.** A farmer wants to plant 65,536 trees in such a way that number of rows must be equal to the number of plants in a row. How many trees will he plant in a row?

    a. 1684
    b. 1268
    c. 668
    d. 256

**37.** How much pay does Mr. Johnson receive if he gives half of his pay to his family, $250 to his landlord, and has exactly 3/7 of his pay left after these expenses?

    a. $3600
    b. $3500
    c. $2800
    d. $1750

**38.** A boy has 4 red, 5 green and 2 yellow balls. He chooses two balls randomly. What is the probability that one is red and other is green?

    a. 2/11
    b. 19/22
    c. 20/121
    d. 9/11

**39. Simplify 5 1/2 − 5 3/7**

   a. 1/10
   b. 1/14
   c. 1/7
   d. 2/7

**40. What is -3 - (-7) - (+5)?**

   a. -6
   b. 6
   c. 3
   d. -1

**41. Solve 3 3/4 x 4/5 x 1 3/4**

   a. 3 3/4
   b. 4 1/3
   c. 6
   d. 5 1/4

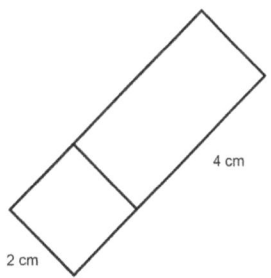

**Note:** figure not drawn to scale

**42. Assuming the smaller shape isa square, what is the perimeter of the above shape?**

    a. 12 cm
    b. 16 cm
    c. 6 cm
    d. 20 cm

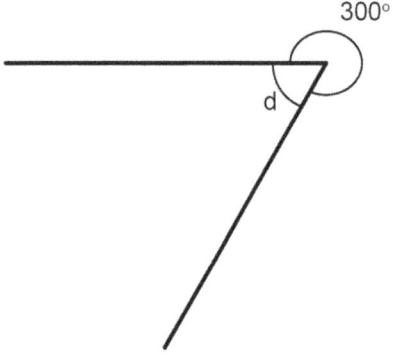

**43. What is the measurement of the indicated angle?**

    a. 45°
    b. 90°
    c. 60°
    d. 50°

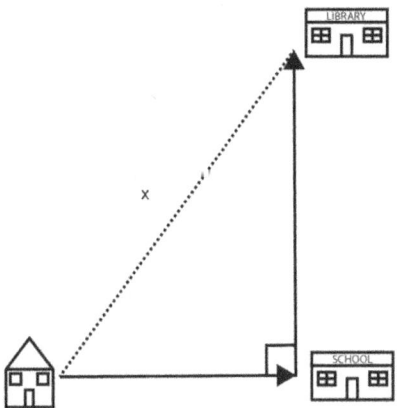

**Note:** figure not drawn to scale

**44. Every day starting from his home Peter travels due east 3 kilometers to the school. After school he travels due north 4 kilometers to the library. What is the distance between Peter's home and the library?**

    a. 15 km

    b. 10 km

    c. 5 km

    d. 12 ½ km

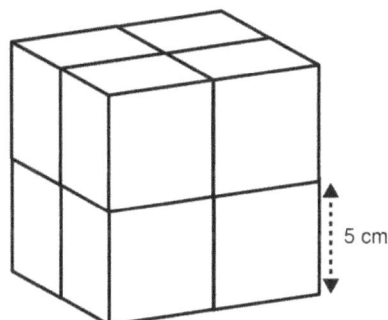

**Note:** figure not drawn to scale

**45. Assuming the figure above is made of cubes, what is the volume?**

    a. 125 cm³
    b. 875 cm³
    c. 1000 cm³
    d. 500 cm³

**46. Solve √121**

    a. 11
    b. 12
    c. 21
    d. None of the above

**47. Write 51.738 to the nearest 100th.**

    a. 51.735
    b. 51.7
    c. 51.73
    d. 51.74

**48. What number is 8 less than 5 squared?**

    a. 22
    b. 17
    c. 19
    d. 21

**49. What is 25 more than 6/8 of 64?**

    a. 73
    b. 85
    c. 55
    d. 62

**50. 1/10 of what number is 5 times 10?**

    a. 150
    b. 500
    c. 250
    d. 400

# Section III - Ability

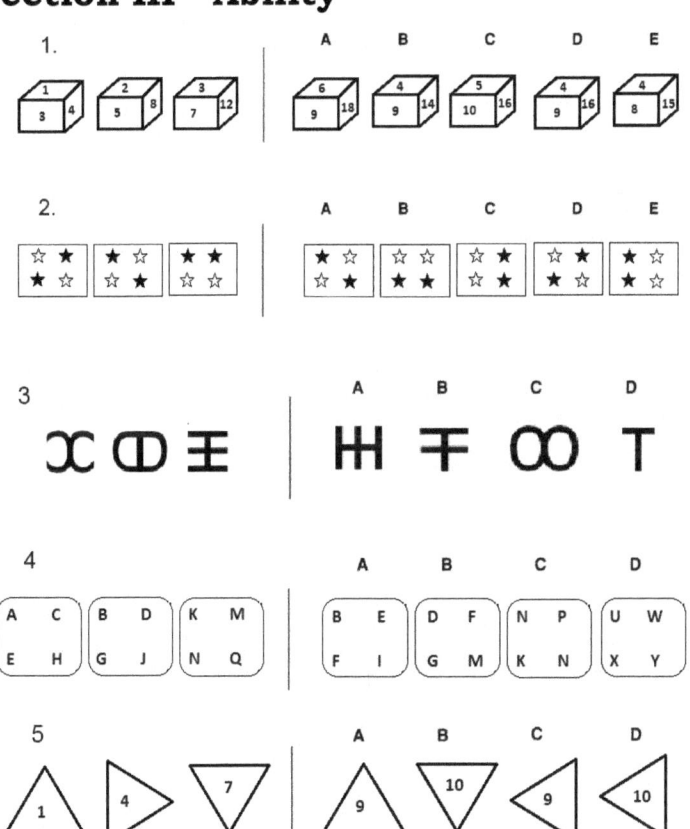

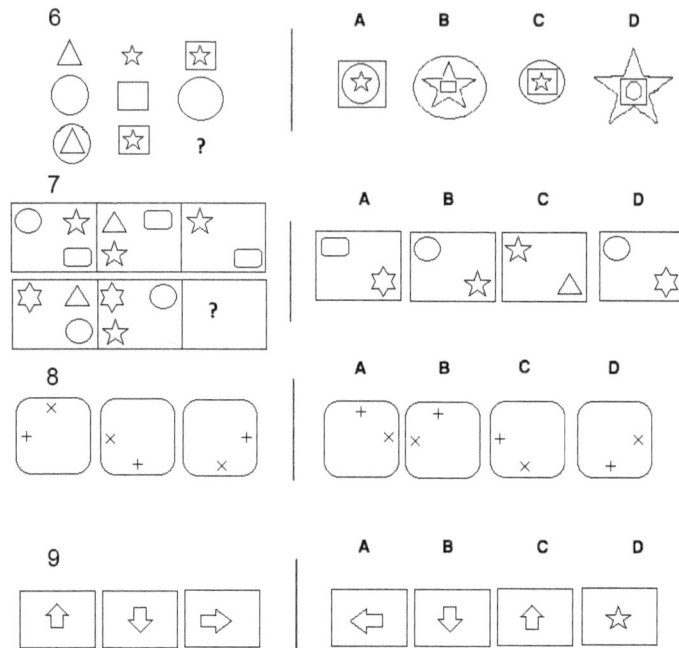

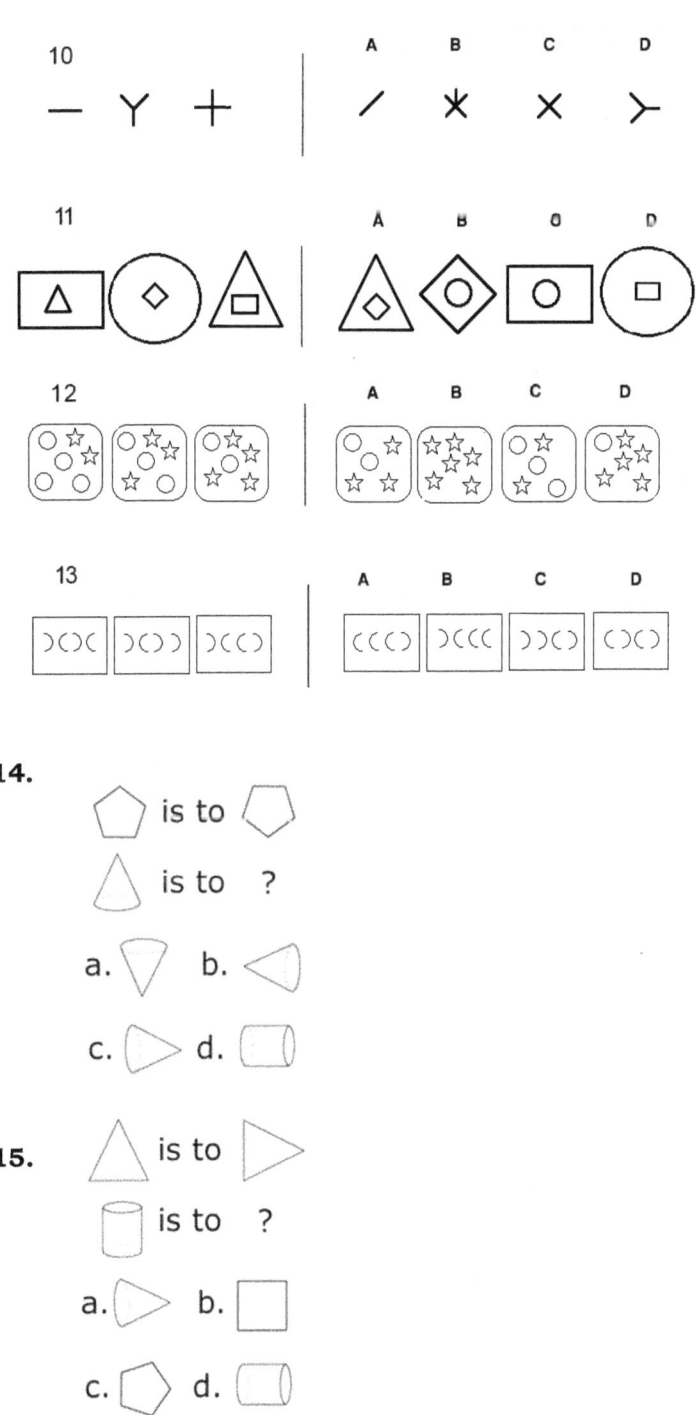

16.

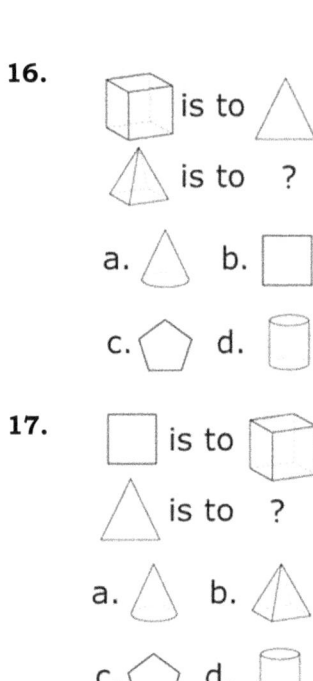

17.

18.

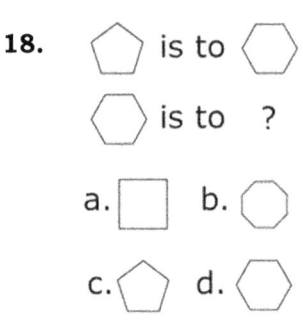

19.

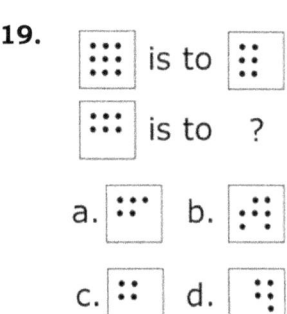

**20.** ▯ is to ▭

   △ is to ?

   a. ▷   b. ⬭

   c. ▷   d. ⌭

**21.** ○ is to ()

   □ is to ?

   a. ▫   b. ▯

**22.** ⊡ is to ⊡

   ⊡ is to ?

   a. ⊡   b. ⊡

   c. ⊡   d. ⊡

**23. When folded along the dotted lines, which shape will you get?**

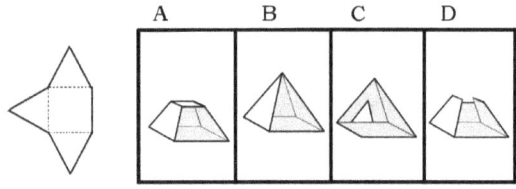

**24. When folded, what pattern is possible?**

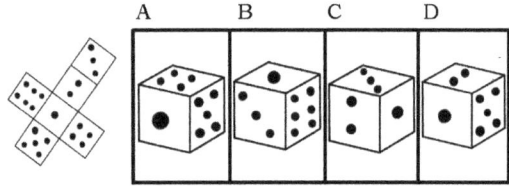

**25. When folded into a loop, what will the strip of paper look like?**

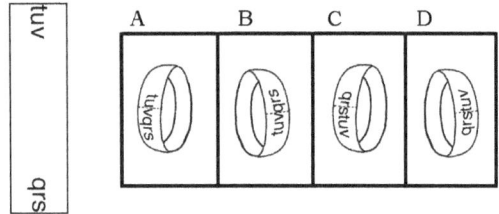

26. Which of the choices is the same pattern at a different angle?

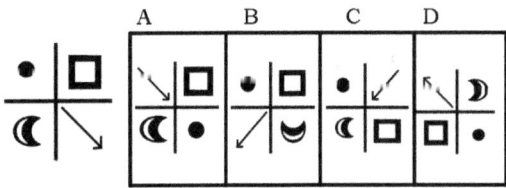

27. When put together, what 3-dimensional shape will you get?

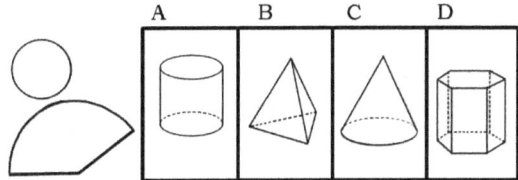

28. When folded, what pattern is possible?

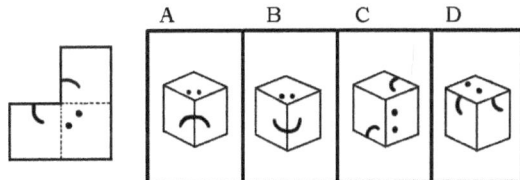

**29. When folded, what pattern is possible?**

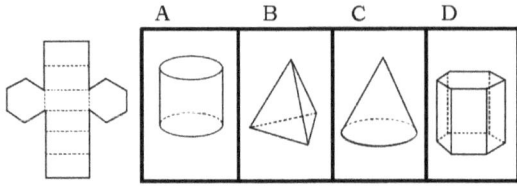

**30. Which of the choices is the same pattern at a different angle?**

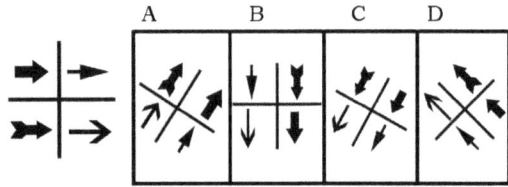

**31. When put together, what 3-dimensional shape will you get?**

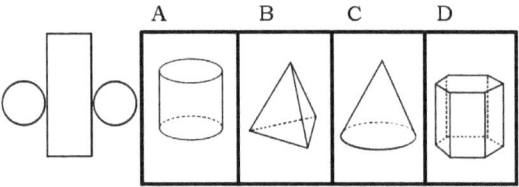

**32. When folded into a loop, what will the strip of paper look like?**

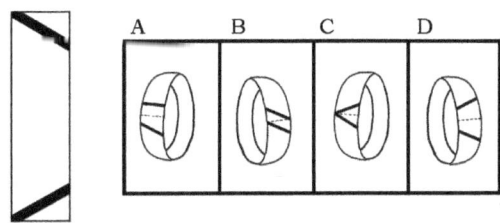

**33. Which of the choices is the same pattern at a different angle?**

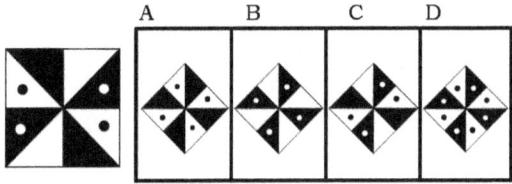

**34. When put together, what 3-dimensional shape will you get?**

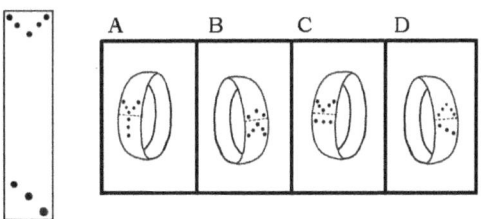

**35. When folded into a loop, what will the strip of paper look like?**

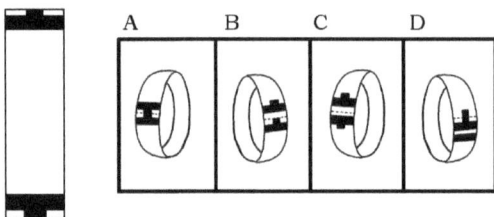

**36. Which of the choices is the same pattern at a different angle?**

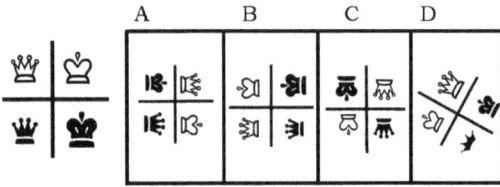

**37. When folded into a loop, what will the strip of paper look like?**

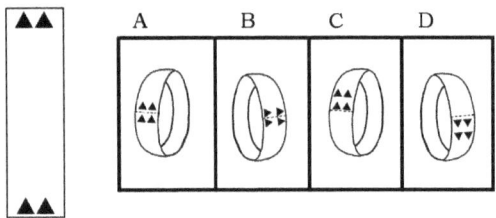

**38. When folded, what pattern is possible?**

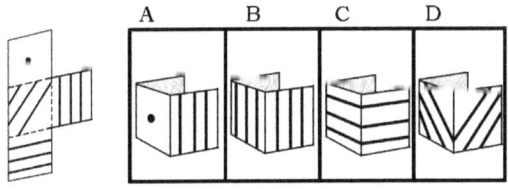

**39. Which of the choices is the same pattern at a different angle?**

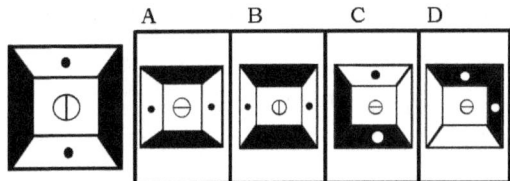

**40. Which of the choices is the same pattern at a different angle?**

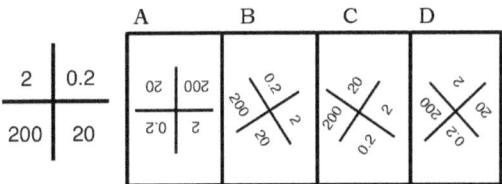

# Answer Key

# Section I Reading

# Part I - Vocabulary

**1. A**
**Intrepid:** Fearless; bold; brave.

**2. B**
**Judicious:** Having, or characterized by, good judgment or sound thinking.

**3. A**
**Negate:** To deny the existence, evidence, or truth of; to contradict.

**4. A**
**Obligatory:** Imposing obligation, morally or legally; binding: an obligatory promise.

**5. B**
**Obsolete:** no longer in use; gone into disuse; disused or neglected.

**6. A**
**Rankle:** To cause irritation or deep bitterness.

**7. C**
**Salient:** Worthy of note; pertinent or relevant.

**8. A**
**Sedentary:** Not moving; relatively still; staying in the vicinity.

**9. A**
**Anonymous:** Of unknown name; whose name is withheld.

**10. A**
**Atrocious:** very bad; abominable or disgusting

**11. D**
**Conclusive:** Providing an end to something; decisive.

**12. C**
**Dupe:** To swindle, deceive, or trick.

**13. D**
**Designate:** appointed; chosen.

**14. B**
**Specious:** adj. Seemingly well-reasoned or factual, but actually fallacious or insincere; strongly held but false.

**15. C**
**Proscribe:** v. To forbid or denounce.

**16. C**
**Veterinarian:** n. A person qualified to treat diseased or injured animals.

**17. C**
**Impeccable:** adj. Perfect, without faults, flaws or errors.

**18. A**
**Boisterous:** adj. Noisy, energetic, and cheerful; rowdy.

**19. B**
**Covert:** adj. Partially hidden, disguised, secret, surreptitious.

**20. B**
**Candid:** adj. Straightforward, open and sincere.

## Part II – Reading Comprehension

**21. B**
We can infer an important part of the respiratory system are the lungs. From the passage, "Molecules of oxygen and carbon dioxide are passively exchanged, by diffusion, between the gaseous external environment and the blood. This exchange process occurs in the alveolar region of the lungs."

Therefore, a primary function of the respiratory system is the exchange of oxygen and carbon dioxide, and this process occurs in the lungs. We can therefore infer that the lungs are an important part of the respiratory system.

**22. C**
The process by which molecules of oxygen and carbon dioxide are passively exchanged is diffusion.

This is a definition type question. Scan the passage for references to "oxygen," "carbon dioxide," or "exchanged."

**23. A**
The organ that plays an important role in gas exchange in amphibians is the skin.

Scan the passage for references to "amphibians," and find the answer.

**24. A**
The three physiological zones of the respiratory system are Conducting, transitional, respiratory zones.

**25. B**
This warranty does not cover a product that you have tried to fix yourself. From paragraph two, "This limited warranty does not cover … any unauthorized disassembly, repair, or modification. "

**26. C**
ABC Electric could either replace or repair the fan, provided the other conditions are met. ABC Electric has the option to repair or replace.

## 27. B
The warranty does not cover a stove damaged in a flood. From the passage, "This limited warranty does not cover any damage to the product from improper installation, accident, abuse, misuse, natural disaster, insufficient or excessive electrical supply, abnormal mechanical or environmental conditions."

A flood is an "abnormal environmental condition," and a natural disaster, so it is not covered.

## 28. A
A missing part is an example of defective workmanship. This is an error made in the manufacturing process. A defective part is not considered workmanship.

## 29. B
The first paragraph tells us that myths are a true account of the remote past.

The second paragraph tells us that, "myths generally take place during a primordial age, when the world was still young, prior to achieving its current form."

Putting these two together, we can infer that humankind used myth to explain how the world was created.

## 30. A
This passage is about different types of stories. First, the passage explains myths, and then compares other types of stories to myths.

## 31. B
From the passage, "Unlike myths, folktales can take place at any time and any place, and the natives do not usually consider them true or sacred."

## 32. B
This passage describes the different categories for traditional stories. The other choices are facts from the passage, not the main idea of the passage. The main idea of a passage will always be the most general statement. For example, choice A, Myths, fables, and folktales are not the same thing, and each describes a specific type of story. This is a true statement from the passage, but not the main idea of the pas-

sage, since the passage also talks about how some cultures may classify a story as a myth and others as a folktale.

The statement, from choice B, Traditional stories can be categorized in different ways by different people, is a more general statement that describes the passage.

### 33. B
Choice B is the best choice, categories that group traditional stories according to certain characteristics.

Choices A and C are false and can be eliminated right away. Choice D is designed to confuse. Choice D may be true, but it is not mentioned in the passage.

### 34. D
The best answer is D, traditional stories themselves are a part of the larger category of folklore, which may also include costumes, gestures, and music.

All the other choices are false. Traditional stories are part of the larger category of Folklore, which includes other things, not the other way around.

### 35. A
There is a distinct difference between a myth and a legend, although both are folktales.

### 36. D
This question tests the reader's summarization skills. The other answers A, B, and C focus on portions of the second paragraph that are too narrow and do not relate to the specific portion of text in question. The complexity of the sentence may mislead students into selecting one of these answers, but rearranging or restating the sentence will lead the reader to the correct answer. In addition, A makes an assumption that may or may not be true about the intentions of the company, B focuses on one product rather than the idea of the products, and C makes an assumption about women that may or may not be true and is not supported by the text.

### 37. B
This question tests reader's attention to detail. If a reader se-

lects A, he or she may have picked up on the use of the word "debate" and assumed, very logically, that the two are at odds because they are fighting; however, this is simply not supported in the text. C also uses very specific quotes from the text, but it rearranges them and gives them false meaning. The artists want to elevate their creations above the creations of other artists, thereby showing that they are "creative" and "innovative." Similarly, D takes phrases straight from the texts and rearranges and confuses them. The artists are described as wanting to be "creative, innovative, individual people," not the women.

**38. A**
This question tests reader's vocabulary and summarization skills. This phrase, used by the author, may seem flippant and dismissive if readers focus on the word "whatever" and misinterpret it as a popular, colloquial terms. In this way, the answers B and C may mislead the reader to selecting one of them by including the terms "unimportant" and "stupid," respectively. D is a similar misreading, but doesn't make sense when the phrase is at the beginning of the passage and the entire passage is on media messages. A is literally and contextually appropriate, and the reader can understand that the author would like to keep the introduction focused on the topic the passage is going to discuss.

**39. A**
This question tests a reader's inference skills. The extreme use of the word "all" in choice B suggests that every single advertising company are working to be approachable, and while this is not only unlikely, the text specifically states that "more" companies have done this, signifying that they have not all participated, even if it's a possibility that they may some day. The use of the limiting word "only" in choice C lends that answer similar problems; women are still buying from companies who do not care about this message, or those companies would not be in business, and the passage specifies that "many" women are worried about media messages, but not all. Readers may find choice D logical, especially if they are looking to make an inference, and while this may be a possibility, the passage does not suggest or discuss this happening. Choice A is correct based on specifically because of the relation between "still working" in the answer and "will

hopefully" and the extensive discussion on companies struggles, which come only with progress, in the text.

### 40. B
The time limit for radar detectors is 14 days. Since you made the purchase 15 days ago, you do not qualify for the guarantee.

### 41. B
Since you made the purchase 10 days ago, you are covered by the guarantee. Since it is an advertised price at a different store, ABC Electric will "beat" the price by 10% of the difference, which is,

500 – 400 = 100 – difference in price

100 X 10% = $10 – 10% of the difference

The advertised lower price is $400. ABC will beat this price by 10% so they will refund $100 + 10 = $110.

### 42. C
The purpose of this passage is to persuade.

### 43. A
We can infer that an important purpose of the circulatory system is that of fighting diseases.

### 44. B
Humans have a closed circulatory system.

### 45. C
Besides blood, the heart and the blood vessels form the cardiovascular system.

### 46. B
The digestive system, along with the circulatory system, helps provide nutrients to keep the human heart pumping.

### 47. C
This question tests the reader's summarization skills. The entire passage is leading up to the idea that the president of the US may not have had grounds to assert his Fourteen Points when other countries had lost so much. A is pretty

directly inferred by the text, but it does not adequately summarize what the entire passage is trying to communicate. B may also be inferred by the passage when it says that the war is "imminent," but it does not represent the entire message, either. The passage does seem to be in praise of FDR, or at least in respect of him, but it does not in any way claim that he is the smartest president, nor does this represent the many other points included. C is then the obvious answer, and most directly relates to the closing sentences which it rewords.

**48. C**
This question tests the reader's attention to detail. The passage does state that A and B are true, and while those statements are in proximity to the explanation for why the war started, they are not the actual reason given. D is a mix up of words used in the passage, which says that the largest powers were in play but not that this fact somehow started the war. The passage does make a direct statement that a domino effect started the war, supporting C as the correct answer.

**49. A**
This question tests the reader's understanding of functions in writing. Throughout the passage, it states that leaders of other nations were hesitant to accept generous or peaceful terms because of the grievances of the war, and the great loss of life was chief among these. While the passage does touch on the devastation of deadly weapons (B), the use of this raw, emotional fact serves a much larger purpose, and the focus of the passage is not the weapons. While readers may indeed consider who lost the most soldiers (C) when so many countries were involved and the inequalities of loss are mentioned in the passage, there is no discussion of this in the passage. D is related to A, But A is more direct and relates more to the passage.

**50. B**
This question tests the reader's vocabulary skills. A may seem appealing to readers because it is phonetically similar to "catalyzed," but the two are not related in any other way. C makes sense in context, but if plugged in to the sentence creates a redundancy that doesn't make sense. D does also

not make sense contextually, even if the reader may consider that funds were needed to create more weaponry, especially if it was advanced.

## Section II - Language

## Part I - Spelling, Capitalization, Punctuation and Usage

**1. D**
The preposition "to" is correct. 'To' here means give.

**2. A**
"Lie" means to recline, and does not take an object. "lay" means to place and does take an object.

**3. A**
Past unreal conditional. Takes the form,
[If ... Past Perfect ..., ... would have + past participle ... ]

**4. B**
This sentence is in the present tense, so "to find" is correct.

**5. A**
Always use the singular verb form for nouns like politics, wages, mathematics, innings, news, advice, summons, furniture, information, poetry, machinery, vacation, scenery etc.

**6. A**
Possessive pronouns ending in 's' take an apostrophe before the 's': one's; everyone's; somebody's, nobody else's, etc.

**7. A**
A bonus is an extra feature, so added is redundant.

**8. D**
When talking about something that didn't happen in the past, use the past perfect (if I had done).

**9. C**
"Lie" means to recline, and does not take an object. "Lay" means to place and does take an object. Peter lay the books on the table (the books are the direct object), or the telephone poles were lying on the road (no direct object).

**10. A**
Titles of short stories are enclosed in quotation marks.

**11. C**
No additional punctuation is required here.

**12. B**
Here the word "sale" is used as a "word" and not as a word in the sentence, so quotation marks are used.

**13. C**
If one of the subjects linked by "either," "or," "nor" or "neither" is in plural form, then the verb should also be in plural, and the verb should be close to the plural subject.

**14. C**
Titles of short stories are enclosed in quotation marks, and commas always go inside quotation marks.

**15. B**
"Ran well" is correct. "Ran good" is never correct.

**16. D**
Commas and periods always go inside quotation marks. Question marks that are part of a quote also go inside quotation marks; however, if the writer quotes a statement as part of a larger question, the question mark is placed after the quotation mark.

**17. C**
Conscientious is the correct spelling.

**18. D**
This is a declarative sentence.

**19. C**
A result is something that occurs at the end, so an 'end result' is redundant.

**20. D**
Both A and C are correct.

> a. Their only employee with a nose ring is a young man named Daniel.
>
> c. Their only employee is a young man with a nose ring named Daniel.

**21. C**
Use a singular verb with either, each, neither, everyone and many.

**22. D**
Leisure is the correct spelling.

**23. C**
Pigeon is the correct spelling.

**24. D**
Odyssey is the correct spelling.

**25. C**
Nouns like deer, sheep, swine, salmon etc can take a singular or plural verb depending if they are used in their singular or plural form.

**26. A**
Use an exclamation mark to end an exclamatory sentence, that is, at the end of a statement showing strong emotion.

**27. D**
Use an exclamation mark after an imperative sentence if the command is urgent and forceful.

**28. D**
**Conclusive** ADJECTIVE providing an end to something; decisive.

**29. A**
'He' is the simple subject of this sentence.

**30. D**
**Deftly:** VERB. Quick and skillful.


# Part II - Paragraphs

**1. A**
Sentence 4 is a fragment. "Which I doubt belongs to any <u>other</u> person."

This sentence is an extension of the sentence preceding it. It does not complete the thought when alone, and is thus a sentence fragment.

**2. A**
Sentence 3 sentence is not consistent with the author's purpose. "For example, for an air stewardess position, girls have to be no more than 163 cm tall; whereas for jobs in foreign affairs, Chinese diplomats are required to match their foreign counterparts."

The passage talks about the people who want to increase their height by undergoing a surgery and points out the minimum height requirements for getting a job that they wish to work in. However, the expression "no more than 163 cm tall" is a statement about a maximum not a minimum. In addition, the sentence refers to Chinese diplomats who must 'match' the height of their foreign counterparts, which could be taller, and hence require surgery, or could be shorter and not require surgery.

**3. B**
The following sentence, if inserted after sentence 7, would best illustrate the main idea of the passage, "This artificial way of gaining height is turning out to be a new trend among the new generation in height conscious China."

The paragraph discusses about the application of leg surgery among Chinese young people to increase their height. This is best reflected in the sentence suggested in choice B which also contributes to the cohesion of the second paragraph as well as allowing a smooth transition between the second and third paragraph.

**4. B**
Suggested changes to sentence 8, "Even parents approve of the idea, being fully aware of all the complications and they are willing to finance such a sophisticated surgery."

The usage of vocabulary is incorrect in this sentence. The word "complexity" is an adjective noun used to describe detailed aspects of a given subject which is less relevant in this case. The word "labyrinth" is also incorrect in this context. The correct counterpart for "complexity" in this case would be "complications" which takes into account the length of the surgery itself and the agony, sacrifice and the commitment associated with it, all in one. Also the word "sophisticated," as suggested in choices B and C in the place of "labyrinth" is more appropriate as it hints about the details of the surgery. Choice B offers both changes.

**5. A**
Sentence 4 is a fragment. "Which I doubt belongs to any other person. "

This sentence is an extension of the sentence preceding it. It does not complete the thought when alone and is thus a sentence fragment.

**6. D**
Sentence 9 is the least relevant to the main idea of the second paragraph. "He is panicked by street dogs and neighbors' cats and to avoid them, he crosses to the other side of the street every now and then."

The second paragraph mainly talks about Luke's odd behavior while in a moving in a crowd, but sentence 9 shifts the subject to his strategy when he encounters cats and dog in the streets.

**7. C**
Sentence 4 contains a redundant phrase. "Which I doubt any other person belongs to other than him."

In this sentence the second "other" is redundant. It can be omitted.

## 8. D
Sentence 5 is a fragment. "Hanging in between two sides of the wall near one corner of the store room which they rarely open, a magnificent piece of art left half woven and still being worked on."

This sentence does not express a complete thought since it does not have a verbal clause. A possible revision would be: "Hanging between two walls near one corner of the store room , lies a magnificent piece of art left half woven and still being worked on."

## 9. B
The following changes to sentence 7 would focus attention on the main idea of the second paragraph, "He is more interested in the web that they weave."

The style of the original sentence lacks cohesion with the passage. Choice B uses a relative comparison with the words "more interested in." The other choices offer changes which does not differ greatly from the original sentence.

## 10. A
Suggested changes to sentence 10 are, "He wonders how they manage to create something unique like this with such a little brain that they have."

The change in this case is related to the use of the word "wander" which is inappropriate in this case. "Wonder" is the correct word in this case.

# Section III – Mathematics

## 1. B
Let XY represent the initial number, $X + Y = 12$, $YX = XY + 36$, only $b = 48$ satisfies both equations.

## 2. A
The problem is to find the perimeter of a shape made by merging a square and a semi circle. Perimeter = 3 sides of

the square + 1/2 circumference of the circle.
= (3 x 5) + ½(5 π)
= 15 + 2.5 π
Perimeter = 17.5 π cm

### 3. B
Volume = Volume of large cylinder - Volume of small cylinder
(Volume of cylinder = area of base x height)
Volume = (π $12^2$x 10) - (π $6^2$x 5), 1440π - 180π
Volume = 1260π $in^3$

### 4. D
We have a circle given with diameter 8 cm and a square located within the circle. We are asked to find the area of the circle for which we only need to know the length of the radius that is the half of the diameter.

Area of circle = π$r^2$ ... r = 8/2 = 4 cm

Area of circle = π * $4^2$

= 16π $cm^2$ ... As we notice, the inner square has no role in this question.

### 5. C
In one trip around the track, he covers the distance equal to the circumference of the circular path.
Circumference of the path = 75 × π = 235.65 meters.
Distance covered in 7 times around = 235.65 × 7 = 1650 meters.

### 6. A
The angles opposite both angles 30° & angle d are respectively equal to vertical angles.
2(30° + d) = 360°
2d = 360° - 60°
2d = 300°
d = 150°

### 7. C
The length of the track = 1.2 km = 1200 meters.
John will complete 1 round in 1200/120 = 10 minutes.
Tony will complete 1 round in 1200/100 = 12 minutes.

David will complete 1 round in 1200/75 = 16 minutes.
The Least Common Multiple of these is 240. Therefore, they will be together after 240 minutes.

**8. D**
1 cm = 5 km so 12.4 cm will be = 12.4 × 5 = 62 km.

**9. B**
Perimeter of a parallelogram is the sum of the sides.

Perimeter = 2(l + b)
Perimeter = 2(3 + 10), 2 x 13
Perimeter = 26 cm

**10. D**
2009 X 108 is 216,972, or approximately 210,000.

**11. D**
First, convert everything to seconds.
Song A = 240 + 56 = 296 sec.
Song B = 120 + 30 = 150 sec.
Song C = 600 + 16 = 616 sec.
Total = 296 + 150 + 616 = 1062. Average will be 1062/3 = 354.
In hours, 354/60 = 5 minutes, 54 seconds.

**12. B**
8.50 * .4 = 3.40 + 1.30 = $4.70

**13. B**
Formula for perimeter of a rectangle is 2(L + W)
p=26, so 2(L+W) = p

The length is 5 inches more than the width, so
2(w+5) + 2w = 26
2w + 10 + 2w = 26
2w + 2w = 26 - 10
4w = 18
**W = 16/4 = 4 inches**
L is 5 inches more than w, so
**L = 5 + 4 = 9 inches.**

**14. D**
Substitute the known variables, (3 x 2) + (4 x 4) x 8 =, 6 + 16 x 8, 24 x 8 = 176

**15. A**
2cnx = 2(4 x 5 x 3)/(2 X 5) =
(2 x 60)/(2 x 5) = 120/10 = 12

**16. A**
First change all the terms to fractions, therefore, we get 7/2 / 14/5, to divide we need to invert the second fraction, 7/2 x 5/14, and then we cancel out to reduce to the lowest terms, 1/2 x 5/2 = 5/4, convert back to proper fraction to get 1 1/4

**17. B**
Substitute known variables, 2 x 9/3 + 3 x 10/5 – 2 =, 18/3 + 30/5 – 2 =, 6 + 6 -2 =, 12 - 2 = 10

**18. A**
First solve the fraction in each bracket separately, therefore (1/3 + 2/6) - (3/4 - 1/3) = (find common denominator) (2+2/6) – (9- 4/12) = (4/6) – (5/12) = (find common denominator again) 8/12 – 5/12 =, 8 - 5/12 = 3/12 = 1/4.

**19. B**
(4/5 - 3/10) + (2/3 – 3/9) =, (find a common denominator) (8-3/10) + (6-3/9) =, (5/10) + (3/9) = 1/2 + 1/3, (find a common denominator) 3+2/6 = 5/6

**20. A**
2 + a number divided by 7.
(2 + X) divided by 7.
(2 + X)/7

**21. D**
Substitute with known variables, (6 x 8) – 12 + (2 x 12) =, 48 – 12 + 24, do the additions first, 48 – (12 + 24) =, 48 – 36 = 12

## 22. C
Subtract the whole numbers and then subtract the fractions, therefore 3 2/3 - 1 2/8 = (3-1) (2/3 − 2/8) = find common denominator to subtract the fractions, (2) (16-6)/24 = 2 10/24, reduce to lowest terms, 2 5/12

## 23. A
Subtract the whole numbers and then subtract the fractions, therefore (7-4) (2/5 − 3/10) = 3 (4-3/10) = 3 1/10

## 24. C
-5 − 5x = 8x + 8, bring same terms to same side of the equation changing the negative or positive signs when they cross over, therefore -5x - 8x = 8 + 5, = -13x = 13, x = 1.

## 25. A
First, convert all the terms to fractions and then cancel out. Therefore, 7/3 x 10/7 x 3/4 = 1/3 x 10/1 x 3/4, 1 x 5 x 1/2, 5 x 1/2 = 2 1/2

## 26. B
Subtract the whole numbers and then subtract the fractions, therefore (7 - 4) (4/5 − 2/3) = 3 (12 - 10/15) = 3 2/15

## 27. C
12x − 8 = 3x + 10, bring same terms to same side of the equation changing the negative or positive signs when they cross over, therefore 12x -3x = 10 + 8, 9x = 18, x = 2

## 28. C
(3/5 - 2/5) + (3/4 − 2/8) =, (3-2/5) + (6-2/8) =, 1/5 + 4/8 =, (find a common denominator) 8+20/40 = 28/40 = 14/20

## 29. D
6a + 4 = 28 + 2a, solve for a. Bring same terms to same side of the equation changing the negative or positive signs when they cross over, therefore 6a − 2a = 28 - 4, 4a = 24, a = 24/4 = 6

## 30. D
(3-1/4) − (3-2/5) =, 3/4 - 1/5 =. 15-4/20 = 11/20

### 31. D
6 + 9x = 12 + 7x, bring same terms to same side of the equation changing the negative or positive signs when they cross over, therefore 9x − 7x = 12 − 6, 2x = 6, x = 6/2, x = 3

### 32. C
First change all the terms to fractions, therefore, we get 32/5 / 16/7, to divide we need to invert the second fraction, 32/5 x 7/16, and then we cancel out to reduce to the lowest terms, 2/5 x 7/1 = 14/5, convert back to proper fraction to get 2 4/5

### 33. B
-6 + 7a = 9 + 4a, bring same terms to same side of the equation changing the negative or positive signs when they cross over, therefore 7a − 4a = 9 + 6 = 3a = 15, a = 15/3, a = 5

### 34. D
As the lawn is square, the length of one side will be= √62500 = 250 meters. Therefore, the perimeters will be 250 × 4 = 1000 meters. The total cost will be 1000 × 5.5 = $5500.

### 35. A
First add all the numbers 3 + 6 + 27 + 13 + 6 + 8 + 12 + 20 + 5 + 10 = 110. Then divide by 10 (the number of data provided) = 110/10 = 11

### 36. D
Let x be number of rows, and number of trees in a row. So equation becomes $X^2$ = 65536, X = 256.

### 37. B
We check the fractions in the question and see that there is a "half" (that is 1/2) and 3/7. So, we multiply the denominators of these fractions to decide how to name the total money. We say that Mr. Johnson has 14x at the beginning; he gives half of this, meaning 7x, to his family. $250 to his landlord. He has 3/7 of his money left. 3/7 of 14x is equal to:

14x * (3/7) = 6x

So,

Spent money is: 7x + 250

Unspent money is: 6x

Total money is: 14x

We write an equation: total money = spent money + unspent money

14x = 7x + 250 + 6x

14x - 7x - 6x = 250

x = 250

We are asked to find the total money that is 14x:

14x = 14 * 250 = $3500

## 38. A
The probability that the 1st ball drawn is red = 4/11. The probability that the 2nd ball drawn is green = 5/10. The combined probability will then be 4/11 X 5/10 = 20/110 = 2/11.

## 39. B
(5-5) (1/2 – 3/7) = (7-6/14) = 1/14

## 40. D
-(-) becomes + and -(+) becomes -, therefore, -3 - (-7) - (+5) = -3 + 7 – 5, -4 + 5 = -1

## 41. D
First, convert all the terms to fractions and then cancel out. Therefore, 15/4 x 4/5 x 7/4 = 3/4 x 4/1 x 7/4, 3/4 x 1/1 x 7/1, 21/4 = 5 1/4

## 42. B
We see that there is a square with side 2 cm and a rectangle adjacent to it, with one side 2 cm (common side with the square) and the other side 4 cm. The perimeter of a shape is found by summing up all sides surrounding the shape, not adding the ones inside the shape. Three 2 cm sides from the square, and two 4 cm sides and one 2 cm side from the rectangle contribute the perimeter.

So, the perimeter of the shape is: 2 + 2 + 2 + 4 + 2 + 4 = 16 cm.

**43. C**
The sum of angles around a point is 360°
d + 300 = 360°
d = 60°

**44. C**
We see that two legs of a right triangle form by Peter's movements and we are asked to find the length of the hypotenuse. We use the Pythagorean Theorem:

Pythagorean Theorem:
(Hypotenuse)$^2$ = (Perpendicular)$^2$ + (Base)$^2$
$h^2 = a^2 + b^2$

Given: $3^2 + 4^2 = h^2$
$h^2$ = 9 + 16
h = $\sqrt{25}$
h = 5

**45. C**
The large cube is made up of 8 smaller cubes with 5 cm sides. The volume of a cube is found by the third power of the length of one side.
Volume of the large cube = Volume of the small cube•8

= (5$^3$)•8 = 125•8

= 1000 cm$^3$

There is another solution for this question. Find the side length of the large cube. There are two cubes rows with 5 cm length for each. So, one side of the large cube is 10 cm.

The volume of this large cube is equal to 10$^3$ = 1000 cm$^3$

**46. A**
$\sqrt{121}$ = 11

**47. D**
The number is 51.738. The last digit is greater than 5, so it is removed and 1 is added to the next number to the left.
Answer = 51.74.

**48. B**
5 X 5 = 25 − 8 = 17

**49. A**
6/8 of 64 = 48 + 25 = 73

**50. B**
5 X 10 = 50
1/10Z = 50
Z = 500

# Section IV - Ability

**1. D**
The numbers on top are increasing by one, the number on the front are increasing by 2 and the numbers on the right are multiple of 4.

**2. B**
Two black stars are placed in the opposite direction to the previous.

**3. B**
These are back to back letters in ascending alphapbetical order.

**4. C**
In the upper row, one letter is missing, and in the bottom row, two letters are missing.

**5. D**
The triangle rotates clockwise and the numbers increase by three.

**6. C**
The first shape should be inside the second shape.

**7. D**
The third box contains two shapes which are present in both of the first two boxes.

**8. A**
The shape rotates counter-clockwise.

**9. A**
The arrow inside the box is the inverse of the previous one.

**10. C**
The number of points increases with each figure.

**11. B**
The larger, exterior figure is the smaller interior figure.

**12. D**
The number of stars increases by one, and the number of circles decreases by one.

**13. C**
The half circles rotate 180 degrees from right to left.

**14. A**
The relation is the same figure rotated.

**15. D**
The relation is the same figure rotated.

**16. B**
The relation is a 3-dimensional figure to a 2-dimensional figure.

**17. B**
The relation is a 2-dimensional figure to a 3-dimentional figure.

**18. B**
The relation is a n-sided figure to an n+1 sided figure.

**19. C**
The first figure has 9 cots in a square and the second figure has 6 dots, which is 1/3 removed.

**20. C**
The relation is a 3-dimentional figure to a rotated 2-dimentional figure.

**21. C**
The relation is the same figure with the bottom half removed.

**22. B**
Each square has the same number of dots inside. Six in the top figures and 5 in the given figure.

**23. B**
**24. A**
**25. D**
**26. D**
**27. C**
**28. B**
**29. D**
**30. C**
**31. A**
**32. C**
**33. C**
**34. D**
**35. A**
**36. B**
**37. A**
**38. C**
**39. A**
**40. A**

# Conclusion

CONGRATULATIONS! You have made it this far because you have applied yourself diligently to practicing for the exam and no doubt improved your potential score considerably! Getting into a good school is a huge step in a journey that might be challenging at times but will be many times more rewarding and fulfilling. That is why being prepared is so important.

**Good Luck!**

## FREE Ebook Version

Download a FREE Ebook version of the publication!

Suitable for tablets, iPad, iPhone, or any smart phone.

**Go to:**
**http://tinyurl.com/ktn9d7v**

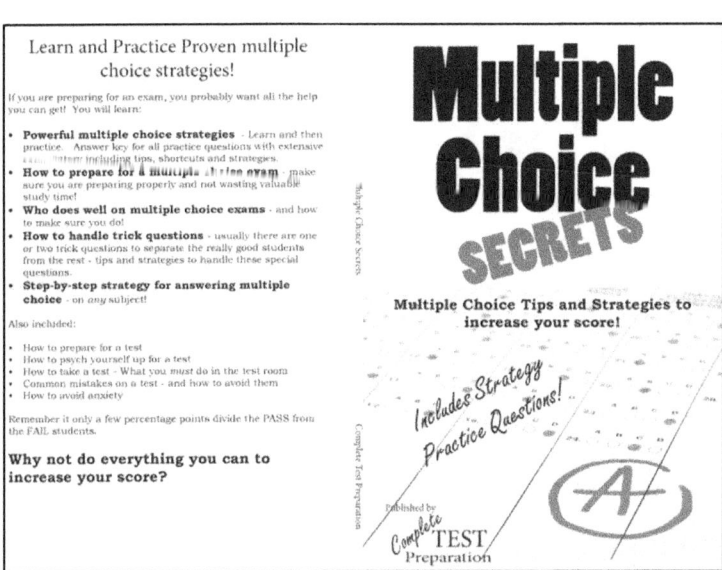

Learn to increase your score using time-tested secrets for answering multiple choice questions!

This practice book has everything you need to know about answering multiple choice questions on a standardized test!

You will learn 12 strategies for answering multiple choice questions and then practice each strategy with over 45 reading comprehension multiple choice questions, with extensive commentary from exam experts!

Maybe you have read this kind of thing before, and maybe feel you don't need it, and you are not sure if you are going to buy this Book.

Remember though, it only a few percentage points divide the PASS from the FAIL students.

Even if our multiple choice strategies increase your score by a few percentage points, isn't that worth it?

www.multiple-choice.ca

www.ingramcontent.com/pod-product-compliance
Lightning Source LLC
LaVergne TN
LVHW010258260326
834688LV00044B/1357